HOW TO WRITE A BOOK IN 90 DAYS GOD'S WAY

Empowering the Christian Writer
To be Heard

Min. Henry Abraham

How To Write A Book In 90 Days God's Way
Empowering The Christian Writer To Be Heard
by Min. Henry Abraham

Printed in the United States of America

ISBN-978-1-60647-150-0

E-mail: Henry@writeitGodsway.com
Website: www.writeitGodsway.com

www.xulonpress.com

Table of Contents

My Heart overflows with a goodly theme;

I address my psalm to a King.

My tongue is like the pen of a ready writer.

—Psalm 45:1 AMP Version (AMP)

The Word Became Flesh...

In The beginning [before all time] was the Word (Christ), and the Word was with God, and the Word was God Himself. [Isa. 9:6]. He was present originally with God. All things were made and came into existence through Him: and without Him was not even one thing made that has come into being. And the Word (Christ) became flesh (human, incarnate) and tabernacled (fixed His tent of flesh, lived awhile) among us: and we [actually] saw His glory (His honor, His majesty), such glory as an only begotten son receives from his father, full of grace (favor, loving-kindness) and truth [Isa. 40:5]

—John 1:1-3, 14 AMP

Prologue

The Bible contains the mind of God, the state of man, the way of Salvation, the doom of sinners and the happiness of believers. The doctrines are holy, the precepts are binding, the histories are true, and its decisions are immutable. Read it to be wise, believe it to be safe, and practice it to be holy. It contains light to direct you, food to support you, and comfort to cheer you. It is the traveler's map, the pilgrim's staff, the pilot's compass, the soldier's sword, and the Christian's charter. Here is Paradise restored, Heaven opened, and the gates of Hell disclosed. Christ is its grand subject, our good its design, and the glory of God its end. It should fill the memory, ruble the heart, and guide the feet. Read it slowly, frequently, and prayerfully. It is a mine of wealth, a paradise of glory, and a river of pleasure. It is given in life, will be opened at the judgment, and will be remembered forever. It involves the highest responsibility, will reward the greatest labor, and will condemn all who trifle with its sacred contents.
—Unknown

How to Use this Book

A re you called to become a Christian writer? If so, you probably find that you are unable to ignore the urge to use your writing to advance the Kingdom of God. You are compelled to put thoughts on paper that can help others examine their beliefs in new ways. You are eager to lead readers to Christ or help believers grow spiritually in new and important ways.

At the heart of your desire, you understand that good writing skills are essential. All too often, an inspired writer begins a promising book, only to give up after that initial burst of energy burns out, leaving an unfinished manuscript that no one will ever read. The writer may lose stamina, be overwhelmed by a hectic schedule, or slow the writing pace to a crawl — and finally stop. You may have a terrific idea that will strengthen others' faith or equip them for ministry. But finding the motivation and momentum to complete your book and prepare it for publication can seem daunting.

This book is designed to encourage writers and guide them to a finished book in 90 days. Sound impossible? This plan is very do-able! Using a speedwriting method bolstered by Scriptural encouragement and journal-based writing exercises, anyone can complete a book in twelve weeks if they take the right steps to make it happen. How can reading this book help you to write yours?

1. Each book chapter guides you through successive steps of the process.
2. A companion workbook helps you understand and apply Biblical principles.
3. Following the Bible reading plan will strengthen your faith.

You will want to clear your schedule of non-essential duties so you will have time to reflect on your topic and write a chapter of your book each week (approximately 2,500 to 3,000 words—about 400 to 500 words daily). Plan to read one book chapter per week, along with daily Scriptural support and workbook exercises. These activities will be the springboard that launches you into a practical development of your book. By the end of twelve weeks, you can complete a twelve-chapter manuscript of approximately 30,000 to 35,000 words (after editing), including the front materials (table of contents, prologue, introduction), and possibly end materials such as the epilogue, index, and/or notes. Within the same period of time or a little more, you can design the book's cover or begin to explore ideas as well as develop a marketing plan and begin to seek pre-publication reviews. But you will have to work consistently at your book project over twelve weeks to make it happen.

Plan to carve a regular or perhaps daily writing time out of your schedule most days of the week. Two to three hours should be enough, depending on how developed your collection of notes, sermon outlines, and rough drafts are, and how quickly you can put your ideas into print. Some readers may have had little or no previous experience or preparation; others will have quite a bit. Everyone should have an idea of the book they want to write, and whom they will write it for. For example, will this be an eight-page preschoolers' book for parents to read to their children? Or will your book be the next 300-page bestselling novel? Maybe you are planning a book on how to revive faith after a lapse of devotion, or a how-to text on jump-starting a ministry or updating a church worship service. Whatever your goal, it is important to have a clear sense of the message you want to share by summarizing it in a paragraph or two.

To get started, use the summary you created to list the main points your book will cover. For a children's inspirational story, you can make these simple and brief, such as helping children to understand that God cares for animals as well as people, and that He expects us to take care of our pets.

For a novel, use a three-part structure to plan your book: 1) introduction of characters, plot, and conflicts; 2) escalation of conflicts as major characters are impacted; and 3) resolution of conflicts and winding down the story to a meaningful conclusion.

For a how-to book, plan your chapters to identify the problem, explore solutions via case studies or examples, and establish principles on which readers can build. This book encourages authors to explore self-publishing options that help writers retain significant control over their own work. Although you certainly can choose to sign a contract with a commercial publisher if one offers suitable terms, that route can be more complicated and time-consuming by the time you find an agent, search for the best possible publishers for your genre of writing, wait for editorial feedback and a publishing decision on your submission, and then start over if your manuscript is rejected. With self-publishing, you learn how to get your words on the printed page and bring them before thousands or even millions of potential readers through a series of basic, easy-to-follow steps. For more information about self-publishing, check out my website at www.writeitGodsway.com.

For copyright information, visit www.copyright.gov.

For information on obtaining a book's bar code, visit www.bowker-barcode.com, where you will become familiar with the four-step process.

Additional self-publishing information can be found in later chapters.

The *Holy Bible* has been translated into many contemporary versions. For purposes of completeness and clarity, this book makes use of the *Amplified Bible,* herein abbreviated as "AMP" following Scriptural references. Copyright (c) 1954 by Zondervan Publising.

As you plan your book-writing adventure, take the following steps to help you get started.

On Your Mark…

1. Pray for God's leading as you prepare to get started; ask Him to guide your work as you study examples of writing styles in the Bible.
2. Organize your writing equipment and materials, including computer, software composing program (like MS Word), paper, and miscellaneous items like stapler, printer cartridge, pens, etc. Be sure to keep a supply of backup items on hand so you won't lose valuable writing time if something should give out unexpectedly.
3. Arrange your schedule for the next 90 days to include daily Bible reading and study with writing time, and be sure to follow through in a consistent manner. Do not let everyday distractions or unnecessary interruptions get in the way of your progress 2 Corinthians 10:4-5 AMP.

Get set…

4. Write a one- to two-paragraph summary of what your book will be about. Keep in mind that good writing should both teach and empower. What will your readers learn? How will you hold their attention and make the information interesting?
5. Create a tentative chapter outline that will become your working table of contents. Be flexible, as chapter titles or content may change as the book undergoes development.
6. Draft a prologue for readers, explaining why you are writing this book and what they can expect to get from it. You may need to discuss effective ways of using your book.

7. Be prepared to give special attention to your daily Bible reading as you study the way it was written and learn how to develop similar techniques for yourself.

GO!

8. Inform family and friends of your writing schedule to invite their support.
9. Begin writing on Day One and keep at it daily, even when you don't feel like it.

As you prepare to take this crucial step to develop your writing ministry, seek God's guidance through prayer so that He can help you go forth and multiply the ideas that will bring readers into closer fellowship with Him.

Foreword

Are you familiar with basic Bible facts? Here is a breakdown of the Bible's structure and themes, according to *The New Expanded Edition: 30 Days to Understanding the Bible in 15 Minutes a Day* (Max Anders, author):

*There are 39 books in the Old Testament, which is the story of God and the Hebrew people, their poets, and their prophets, in the following genres:

1. historical
2. poetical
3. prophetical

*There are 27 books in the New Testament, which is the story of Jesus of Nazareth, the church He founded, and its growth under the leadership of His Apostles after His death. .

1. historical
2. Pauline
3. general

*There are 66 books in the entire Bible.

In the first decade of the 21ˢᵗ century, Christian books are proliferating. Christian publishing in general has grown by leaps and bounds over the past twenty years, and Christian titles in particular can be found in abundance at all major chain and independent bookstores across the nation and even around the world. The success of fantasy books like *The Fall of Lucifer* by Wendy Alec, and *The Lion, the Witch, and the Wardrobe* by C.

S. Lewis have paved the way for similar works for a new generation. The *Left Behind* series, along with fiction by Frank Peretti and a host of other accomplished authors underscore the public's interest in Christian material. Publishing trends as reported in the industry magazines and surveys now reveal ongoing growing interest in Biblical topics and a subsequent growth in reader demand for these products. There has never been a better time to become a Christian author.

How to Write a Book in 90 Days God's Way provides inspiration and guidance for the novice author who is struggling to complete a book in a timely manner, or the seasoned author who must write on a tight deadline against competing priorities. This book can help writers achieve their goals by learning how to write routinely, how to examine their goals and motives, and how to consider potential readers, a marketing niche, and commercial vs. self-publishing options.

I have tried to craft a caring and compassion book that guides writers through the focusing, drafting, and revising stages of completing a book. Setting professional goals and writing on a schedule can help even the most unsure author to complete a book-length manuscript in 90 days—while doing it God's way.

For writers who seek expert assistance and a plan for meeting their publishing goals, this book offers information and resources to help you get started and stay on track. Authoring a book is a God-given talent. If you feel called to this ministry, don't give up. Let my insight and experience serve your interests by helping you to develop a book in 90 days—God's way. Visit my website at www.writeitGodsway.com.

My Commitment

With God's guidance, I dedicate the next 90 days of my life to writing an inspired book manuscript while studying His Word to understand God's plan for my writing talent.

_____

Print Name

_____

Sign Name

Roll your works upon the Lord [commit and trust them wholly to Him;
He will cause your thoughts to become agreeable to His will,
and] so shall your plans be established and succeed.
—Proverbs 16:3 AMP

Acknowledgements

T his book is first and foremost dedicated to the Lord God Almighty Jesus Christ. His power and guidance have been instrumental in forming the seeds of ideas that have sprung to life in published form.

I also would like to thank the readers of this book who, by applying its principles in writing to their own books, will fulfill God's purposes for their lives in doing the work of our Heavenly Father.

To my virtuous wife Katrina, son Johnivan, Harry Abraham III, Harry Abraham, Sr., my lovely mother who prayed for me when I couldn't pray for myself, the late Olivia Abraham, and to my pastor and spiritual father Dr. Bill Winston for all of the wonderful teachings you continue to give. To all the aspiring Christian writers, believe me with God, you can do it! (Phil. 4:13 AMP)

How to Write a Book in 90 Days God's Way owes its finished form to the professionals at Xulon Publishing, David, and Debra, my God-sent graphic artist and editor, whose expertise helped to create the finished book that we hope to make available wherever aspiring writers can make use of it to advance the Kingdom of God in excellence and integrity.

In the service of the King
Henry Abraham

Introduction

God: The Ultimate Author

*"Every Scripture is God-breathed (given by His inspiration) and profit-
able for instruction, for reproof and conviction of sin, for correction of
error and discipline in obedience, [and] for training in righteousness
(in holy living, in conformity to God's will in thought, purpose, and
action)..."*
—2 Timothy 3:16 AMP

S o you're ready to become an author! Writing can be an extremely satisfying and meaningful ministry. But each article or book that you author
requires thoughtful consideration. Are you writing a book to please God or
to satisfy yourself? Many writers desire the fame and riches offered by this
world. Eager to see their name in print and their book on store shelves, they
may surrender to the voice of temptation suggesting they capitalize on sex
and violence to attract a secular audience and earn impressive royalties.

Christian writers create a book because they hope it will glorify God.
They have an inspired message to share that can build faith, remove doubts,
and pave the road to salvation or spiritual growth. Yet, authors who seek
to inspire others will themselves require inspiration. Even though there
are plenty of inspirational books readily available through a variety of
purchasing media, Christians need look no further than the Bible for
models of written excellence and spiritual encouragement.

The Bible is God's Book to humans living on this earth. Published
serially over thousands of years by at least forty contributing authors, the
Scriptures were penned by authors inspired by the Holy Spirit to share

God's message of creation, judgment, promise, and salvation to those who read His Word. Just as you hope that people will read your book, so God wants us to read the Bible to see what He wants to tell us:

> *"Study and be eager and do your utmost to present yourself to God approved (tested by trial), a workman who has no cause to be ashamed, correctly analyzing and accurately dividing (rightly handling and skillfully teaching) the Word of Truth."*
> *—2 Timothy 2:15 AMP*

> *"And how from your childhood you have had a knowledge of and been acquainted with the sacred Writings, which are able to instruct you and give you the understanding for salvation which comes through faith in Christ Jesus [through the leaning of the entire human personality on God in Christ Jesus in absolute trust and confidence in His power, wisdom, and goodness.].*

> *Every Scripture is God-breathed (given by His inspiration) and profitable for instruction, for reproof and conviction of sin, for correction of error and discipline in obedience, [and] for training in righteousness (in holy living, in conformity to God's will in thought, purpose, and action).*

> *So that the man of God may be complete and proficient, well fitted and thoroughly equipped for every good work."*
> *—2 Timothy 3:15-17 AMP*

As you plan your book's message, give thought to the ways in which God's Word shares eternal truths with readers past, present, and future. The Bible offers many examples of Christianity's timeless messages. In the Old Testament, several types of personal and factual writing can be found:

1 Stories of Bible figures in conflict with God and each other
2 Legal descriptions of real and personal property
3 Songs of triumph and sorrow
4 Poems celebrating God's goodness and human frailties
5 Wise sayings for instruction and guidance
6 Historical biographies and chronologies
7 Prophecies

The New Testament likewise offers God's truth through meaningful literary conventions:

1 Genealogies
2 Guidelines
3 Parables
4 Dialogue
5 Letters
6 Visionary revelation
7 Rhetoric and persuasion

Jesus used writing when He stooped and wrote something in the sand when the adulterous woman was brought to Him for judgment. While we don't know what was written, His words may have convicted the hypocrites before Him, as they left in silence, perhaps shamed by Jesus' unspoken communication as well as His pronouncement that the one without sin should cast the first stone. What did Jesus write in the sand that day?

> *"But Jesus went to the Mount of Olives.*
> *Early in the morning (at dawn), He came back into the temple (court), and the people came to Him in crowds. He sat down and was teaching them,*
> *When the scribes and Pharisees brought a woman who had been caught in adultery. They made her stand in the middle of the court and put the case before Him.*
> *'Teacher,' they said, 'This woman has been caught in the very act of adultery.*
> *'Now Moses in the Law commanded us that such [women— offenders] shall be stoned to death. But what do You say [to do with her—what is Your sentence?'*
> *[Deut. 22:22-24.]*
> *This they said to try (test) Him, hoping they might find a charge on which to accuse Him. But Jesus stooped down and wrote on the ground with His finger.*
> *However, when they persisted with their question, He raised Himself up and said, 'Let him who is without sin among you be the first to throw a stone at her.'*

Then He bent down and went on writing on the ground with His finger.

They listened to Him, and then they began going out, conscience-stricken, one by one, from the oldest down to the last one of them, till Jesus was left alone, with the woman standing there before Him in the center of the court.

When Jesus raised Himself up, He said to her, 'Woman, where are your accusers? Has no man condemned you?'

She answered, 'No one, Lord!' And Jesus said, 'I do not condemn you either. Go on your way and from now on sin no more.'"
—John 8:1-11 AMP

Furthermore, Jesus' life inspired the disciples to write the four Gospels as well as several epistles that were used to emphasize or explain Christ's ministry and the Christian life. Clearly, the written word served as one of God's most effective tools in preaching the Gospel to the entire world since Jesus issued the Great Commission and ascended into Heaven. Without the recorded Word of God, it would be impossible to understand God's purpose and discern His character through the words of prophets and ministers. The Bible is a recording of divine revelation and inspired events. Published in millions of copies to innumerable languages in a variety of versions that help readers of all backgrounds to understand the Bible's meaning, the Word of God provides ongoing inspiration and hope to readers around the world today.

God provides Christian authors with the gift and skill to guide spiritual behavior and inspire our ministries through the written word. For some, that involves writing about Christian values in fictional stories that offer didactic perspectives or realistic insights. Others teach valuable lessons or offer thoughtful insights in their works of non-fiction. If you feel that God is leading you to write for His glory, this book can help. If you are prepared to write a book in 90 days, do it God's way. Stay focused on Him by following the 90-day Bible reading plan at the back of this book. Make a commitment to read a chapter of this book each week and do the accompanying exercises as motivation for meeting your writing goals. If you get behind, do what you can to catch up to reach your goal in 90 days. But if that is not possible, simply pick up where you left off and continue your journey, extending the finish time, as needed:

"Do you not know that in a race all the runners compete, but [only] one receives the prize? So run [your race] that you may lay hold [of the prize] and make it yours.

Now every athlete who goes into training conducts himself temperately and restricts himself in all things. They do it to win a wreath that will soon wither, but we [do it to receive a crown of eternal blessedness] that cannot wither.

Therefore I do not run uncertainly (without definite aim). I do not box like one beating the air and striking without an adversary.

But [like a boxer] I buffet my body [handle it roughly, discipline it by hardships] and subdue it, for fear that after proclaiming to others the Gospel and things pertaining to it, I myself should become unfit [not stand the test, be unapproved and rejected as a counterfeit].

— 1 Corinthians 9:24-27 AMP

First Things First: Consecrate Your Writing

If you are sincere about becoming a Christian writer, seek God's will and His direction. Meditate on Bible verses like the following to draw closer to the Lord, and pray for spiritual guidance each day.

"Lean on, trust in, and be confident in the Lord with all your heart and mind and do not rely on your own insight or understanding."
— Proverbs 3:5 AMP
"But seek (aim at and strive after) first of all His kingdom and His righteousness (His way of doing and being right), and then all these things taken together will be given you besides."
— Matthew 6:33 AMP

Write a prayer of worship, confession, repentance, and petition, and read it during your personal devotions with God. Ask Him to open or close doors that will lead you through the maze of discovery in understanding His plan for your life. If you are meant to write, nothing will prevent it. If God has another plan for you, seeking publication means that you do it minus His blessing or protection. (See Appendix for sample Writer's Prayer)

It is good to give the Lord a tithe of your earnings from book-related income. Although it may seem premature to discuss profits, a good steward plans earnings to avoid uncontrolled spending and waste. Give Him the first fruits of each day, spending time in Bible reading, worship, and prayer. Only then will you be truly inspired, committed, and ready to write in accordance with His divine plan for your life.

—Malachi 3:8-12 AMP:

"'Will a man rob or defraud God? Yet you rob and defraud Me.'

But you say, 'In what way do we rob or defraud You?' [You have withheld your) tithes and offerings.

'You are cursed with the curse, for you are robbing Me, even this whole nation' [Lev. 26:14-17]

'Bring all the tithes (the whole tenth of your income) into the storehouse, that there may be food in My house and prove Me now by it, says the Lord of hosts, 'if I will not open the windows of heaven for you and pour you out a blessing, that there shall not be room enough to receive it.' [Mal. 2:2]

'And I will rebuke the devourer [insects and plagues] for your sakes and he shall not destroy the fruits of your ground, neither shall your vine drops its fruit before the time in the field,' says the Lord of hosts.

'And all nations shall call you happy and blessed, for you shall be a land of delight,' says the Lord of hosts."

This book comes with a 90-day Bible reading plan that will help you read through the entire New Testament in the same period of time as you are writing your book. Reading the Bible will provide insight to Scriptural inspiration and examples. Also available is a companion workbook and other writer's resources that are designed to help improve your writing by completing daily short activities. With this plan you will be spiritually nurtured even as you write your book to nurture others:

"Then He [thoroughly] opened up their minds to understand the Scriptures,..."
—Luke 24:45 AMP

Doing things God's way ensures the best chance of ultimate success. Get ready to unburden your heart through spiritual insight and creativity over the next 90 days!

> *"And though your beginning was small, yet your latter end would greatly increase."*
—*Job 8:7 AMP*

Chapter One

Getting Started

"I [the Lord] will instruct you and teach you in the way you should go;
I will counsel you with My eye upon you."
—Psalm 32:8 AMP

When you think about King David, have you ever wondered how a man with much human blood on his hands, at one time considered the enemy of the people when pursued by King Saul, and later temporarily ousted by his beloved son Absalom, could be considered "a man after God's own heart"? How did David's spiritual life counter all his problems and sins from youth on up? How could God so greatly love a murderer, adulterer, negligent parent, and polygamist to grant David the throne of Israel and his descendents forever if they would keep God's commandments? The Bible has answers to questions like these that can help us better understand the mind of God in choosing who He will love and who He will reject. Although Saul was Israel's first king and was initially consecrated to God, Saul did not stay loyal to His Creator:

> *"But now your kingdom shall not continue: the Lord has sought out [David] a man after His own heart, and the Lord has commanded him to be prince and ruler over His people, because you have not kept what the Lord commanded you."*
> *—1 Samuel 13:14 AMP*

That is still the problem today. People consistently refuse to obey God. Beginning with David's son Solomon, who duplicated his father's sins and added more of his own, including idolatry, David's descendents broke faith with God. They committed increasingly vile, sinful acts until God turned them over to their enemies, the Babylonians, who forced them into foreign exile. But why was David so special? No other ruler earned God's favor as David did.

A clue can be found in the Psalms. David's life is narrated in the Books of First and Second Samuel, First and Second Kings, and First and Second Chronicles, and he himself penned dozens of Psalms dedicated to the Lord. As you read his words of fear, failure, praise, and triumph, you will find revealed a man who truly loved God above all else—even more than friends, wives, and children. He was committed to serving the one true God of Israel and everyone throughout the region—enemies included— knew it. Most respected him for it. And their awareness stemmed to a great degree from the Psalms that David wrote to honor and praise his Lord, some of which were emotive, others prophetic, but all revealing a depth of character that demonstrated a life of unshakable faith. Those famous lines penned thousands of years ago greatly amazed, inspired, and encouraged the people of Israel and surrounding nations. They remain a moving testimony to God's merciful, just, and forgiving nature. Today, people who are in despair, suffering from illness or on their deathbed take comfort from the Psalms. David's writing has stood the test of time and has carried God's will to numerous generations. Will yours follow a similar path?

"I will give to the Lord the thanks due to His rightness and justice,
and I will sing praise to the name of the Lord Most High."
—Psalm 7:17 AMP

Thankfully, most of us don't have to worry about vengeful kings or cruel enemies pursuing us with murder in their hearts. Our thoughts are occupied with reaching goals and earning success. We worry about jobs, families, and homes. We strive for popularity, status, and superiority. Were these David's goals? No. He simply followed where God led and was showered with amazing grace in all areas of his life. His career path took him from a shepherd of sheep to a leader of people. David was a great ruler who left a mighty legacy. Despite committing some serious sins that disappointed God and wounded or destroyed others, David remained a man after God's own heart. How would it feel to be remembered in this way?

If you are a Christian whose eternal hope is secure in Christ, then you undoubtedly make it a point to process your long-term goals as well as daily decisions through the Word of God and frequent prayer. And that is how you will begin this purposeful journey toward sharing a message with future readers. If you plan to write a non-fiction book, then probably you will choose a how-to approach by offering advice, guidance, or principles based on personal insight and biblical study. But if you prefer writing a fictional novel, you will want to tell a gripping story with life-like characters that share a message of hope.

If you have read this book's Prologue and Introduction, hopefully by now you have prepared a summary of your book's goal and main points, and are ready to begin the process of developing a publishable manuscript during the next twelve weeks. When you finish reading this chapter, take some time to read this week's Bible reading plan at the end of each chapter in this book and do the writing exercises for Week One. Soon, you will be on your way to completing an inspirational work of art that may become a mighty tool for crafting Christian values in the lives of your readers:

"In the morning You hear my voice, O Lord; in the morning I prepare [a prayer, a sacrifice] for You and watch and wait [for You to speak to my heart]."
—Psalm 5:3 AMP

Let God Lead

Although you may be tempted to run ahead with your plan as creativity begins to flow, the wise person who writes a book God's way will first seek His leading. In working through the writing activities that will build your book, remember to pray first and write second. Meditate on God's Word not only for its message, but on the way it is designed to have a specific impact on endless generations of readers. Ask God to guide your thoughts and words in the direction He wants them to go. Faithfully confess Jesus as Savior, and watch exciting things begin to happen in your writing as well as your personal life!

"This Book of the Law shall not depart out of your mouth, but you shall meditate on it day and night, that you may observe and do according to all that is written in it. For then you shall make your

way prosperous, and then you shall deal wisely and have good success."
—*Joshua 1:8 AMP*

Before moving on to discuss your book's development, below is an overview of non-fiction and fiction writing guidelines. Understanding the style and principles of both types of writing will help to guide the progress of your book so that it follows traditional literary styles and can be well understood and appreciated by experienced readers.

What is Non-Fiction?

Non-fiction writing discusses factual ideas, experiences, and plans, most often from a problem-solving approach. There are non-fiction books on how to get wealthy, healthy, happy, and wise, along with how-to approaches for just about anything a person might want to learn, such as cooking, exercising, skydiving, or woodworking. Books have been written on abstract ideas, like understanding the universe or the meaning of patriotism, as well as on concrete concepts, like housebreaking a puppy. If you have useful information that could benefit others who are willing to consider you a reliable expert, then a non-fiction book is a good choice for your message. Readers will expect your writing to be clear, focused, and directional. Christian non-fiction falls into several genres, or categories, like these:

1   Self-help (better devotions, improving your marriage, etc.)
2   How to do something better (witness, evangelize, minister, grow a church, etc.)
3   Sharing insight (pastoral pressures, single parenthood, chaste living, etc.)
4   Offering advice (being a trustworthy friend, overcoming a bad habit, etc.)
5   Biographies and autobiographies (memoirs)

Most of us have accumulated various life experiences, some of which we've mastered better than others. For example, you might have great ideas for living on a tight budget but have no clue about preparing a high school student to succeed in college. Some of the best lessons we learn in life come from losses and failures, as evidenced in Elisabeth Elliot's book *Through Gates of Splendor* that describes the murder of missionary husband Jim Elliot by Ecuador Indians. Tragedies can serve as sources of inspiration to share with others via the written word.

Typically, a non-fiction book will be based on a main idea that can interest and possibly benefit readers in some way. Your message may build on an old or existing idea by adding a unique, new twist. An example would be taking the well-established idea of having a daily devotional and tweaking it by adding your experience or creativity to suggest, for example, that one should meditate on God's creation before daily devotions, and then explaining how to do this, along with potential benefits.

Non-Fiction Guidelines

Your information should be clear and easy for readers to apply. Generally, it's a good idea to break up complex ideas into smaller paragraphs, each with its own point that helps to develop the main idea, called the thesis. Start with an overview of your primary point, develop it with explanation and examples, and then conclude with a powerful finish that reiterates the main idea or offers a principle for its application. Use everyday language and a simple style to hold your readers' attention.

1. Write the book around a main concept. This should be the theme or message that you want to share with readers. For example, to encourage readers to establish a personal ministry, the title and introduction will explain why that's important and how the book will help them accomplish it.
2. Each chapter should develop one piece or angle of the big idea. To extend the example in the first point above, each chapter could suggest principles to help readers start their personal ministries. Each chapter might have guidelines, examples, and perhaps illustrations.
3. The book should offer Biblical content. This may involve research, revelation, knowledge, or the author's experience and observation. By the time readers finish reading, they will have some ideas for beginning a personal ministry and perhaps be ready to start.

The purpose of a non-fiction book is to educate people about your topic and equip them with knowledge about applying your book's information to their own lives for understanding or profit. For Christians, non-fiction often is centered on God's Word in offering principles that can strengthen faith or equip them for a Christ-centered life spent in service to Him and others.

> *"The reverent and worshipful fear of the Lord is the beginning and the principal and choice part of knowledge [its starting point and its essence]; but fools despise skillful and godly Wisdom, instruction, and discipline. [Ps. 111:10.]"*
> —*Proverbs 1:7 AMP*

What is Fiction?

Fiction means simply telling a story. The story may be completely imagined, or it can be based on real events that have been rearranged or embroidered to keep the story more fictional than true.

There are many types of fiction, such as short stories, fables, parables, novels, and romances. There are also several genres, or styles of fiction, each with its own convention:

1   Historical romance
2   Contemporary romance
3   Action / adventure
4   Suspense / thriller
5   Fantasy / science fiction
6   Young adult (middle school through high school)
7   Children's picture books / story books
8   Westerns
9   Animal stories

Each of these categories can be broken down into further subcategories to more specifically pinpoint a story's genre. For example, a historical romance might be further refined to a Renaissance or Regency romance. Contemporary romance can include Christian contemporary, urban, or "chick lit", among others.

It is important to decide which genre and sub-genre your book most closely fits. Then learn all you can about that category to ensure you understand its conventions and style. Browse samples in the library or bookstore, and read about the style online in book or literary blogs and websites. This will help you write your book in a similar way. Readers who are in the market for a book of a particular type typically look for books that are written by a certain author, or a new author whose style resembles a beloved previous author. In fact, many bookstores and book-selling websites specialize in one or more genres or sub-genres, so you will need to classify your book before choosing a marketing plan, agent, or bookseller. If you plan to consider marketing your book to a commercial publishing house, it is important to understand that editors at a publishing company may want to know the titles of other books (preferably from their published works) that your book is most like. For help with getting your book into readers' hands, visit my website to learn more about *How to Market a Book in 90 Days God's Way.*

Avoid claiming that your book is different from everything else on the market, as many publishers want to work with books that fit in with others of its kind. Readers are always looking for new authors in their favorite reading styles, so it is a good thing for your book to be somewhat like those sitting on bookshelves rather than in a league of its own. If your book is too different, it may be difficult for an agent, distributor, or publisher to explain your book to potential readers and stir enough interest to sell it.

A long-time recommendation for authors is to write what you know. If you are a fan of a particular writing genre or style, chances are you will want to write your book to fit in that category because you are already familiar with its type. But if you prefer to experiment with new styles or genres of writing, at least be sure to understand its conventions and how it will affect your marketing of the book so that you can arrange the contents accordingly.

Literary Conventions

Whether you write fiction or non-fiction, hopefully you have done plenty of reading before writing your own book. Most famous authors are notorious readers of a wide selection of classic works and pop best sellers from which they have drawn unique inspiration. The Bible and Shakespeare are two of the most popular, longstanding sources in Western civilization. If you haven't read these works, you should plan on doing so in the near future. You also should become familiar with world literature by authors from around the globe and a variety of time periods, themes, and locations.

This writing plan comes with a 90-day schedule for reading the New Testament. Not only will readers find Scripture inspiring, but they also will find it instructional for learning classical rhetorical modes that have continued to influence generations of readers. If you can learn to read the Bible on a daily basis, understand its precepts, and apply Scriptural principles to your life, you can enhance your chances of getting your own book written and published because of 1) following the Bible's literary examples and styles, and 2) seeking God through His Word to line up your desires with His Will for your life:

> *"Even so, every healthy (sound) tree bears good fruit [worthy of admiration], but the sickly (decaying, worthless) tree bears bad (worthless) fruit."*
> —*Matthew 7:17 AMP*

Here are some of the most popular writing conventions to enhance either fiction or non-fiction writing.

Fiction Guidelines:
1. **Plot.** All fictional writing, whether a short story or a novel, should follow a plot, or plan, that reveals the story through each chapter. The plot may be straightforward by starting at a point of introduction, creating conflicts that heighten to a critical climax, and then resolve to a satisfying if nail-biting finish. Other plot options include the flashback technique, where the narrative jumps back in time, or a flash-forward technique, when the story goes into the future temporarily. Some narratives skip from one main character to the next in round-robin fashion to give readers the benefit of multiple perspectives.

2. **Narrator.** Someone has to relay the events of the story. Sometimes this is a narrator who may be "omniscient," that is, someone who knows what the characters are thinking and details that are revealed as the story is told. One of the characters may be the narrator, so the story is explained from the first-person perspective of "I" or "we," if the narrator represents a group of people, like a family, a couple, or even a town. The narrator may be unreliable, as in the writing of Edgar Allan Poe, due to mental instability or substance abuse. A narrator can be a character in the story, the author, or an impersonal authorial voice.

3. **Conflicts.** All fiction pivots on intriguing conflicts between the story's characters. These are the most common or universal conflicts found throughout Western literature:

1 Man vs. God
2 Man vs. self
3 Man vs. nature
4 Man vs. society
5 Man vs. man
6 Man vs. woman
7 Man vs. technology
8 Man vs. satan

One or more of these should be present in the story to make it exciting and lead to action.

4. **Characters.** A character-driven story involves one or more central characters on which the focus is centered. The Batman movies are a good example of character-driven stories, because they evolve from the main figure of the superhero. The traditional good guy vs. bad guy motif continues to be popular today. There also may be stereotypical figures of the messiah, a commonplace person who sacrifices his life for the safety of others. The dark stranger is someone who is mysterious and usually brings an element of mystery or danger to the plot. The dark woman can be a seductive lady with a questionable past who is destroyed because of her inability to escape a sinful lifestyle or because of efforts to corrupt a decent man. A "satan" figure is the embodiment of evil or temptation, and may take different forms.

5. **Symbols.** Symbols are numbers, names, colors, or tangible objects that reflect some hidden or secondary meaning to the story. For example, Nathaniel Hawthorne's *The Scarlet Letter* uses the "A" sewn into Hester Prynne's dress to symbolize her sin publicly to the colony in which she lives. The numbers 3 and 7 often have religious or Biblical significance, while colors like white represent purity or sterility, red signifies passion or hell, and pink may denote innocence. A river might have feminine connotations, as do mountains or other types of geographical terrain.

41

6. **Figurative language.** The use of similes, metaphors, hyperbole, synecdoche, personification, alliteration, and other literary conventions can make story telling more lyrical and thought provoking. Even parallel structure, analogy, repetition, and other devices can dress up common phrasing to make it decorous, if the writer uses such devices skillfully to enhance the ideas behind the writing.

7. **Tone or mood.** It is important for every story to establish a mood, or tone. This helps to create an environment where readers have a sense of what to expect, such as mystery, suspense, nostalgia, romance, fantasy, or adventure. Creating a mood can be achieved through description, word choices, and language style. Furthermore, circumstances, characters, and plot also have a bearing on the mood of the story.

8. **Setting.** The location, or setting, of a story plays a crucial role. Setting can suggest a literal location, such as Chicago, Illinois, as well as a specific time period, say, the Civil War. Setting also can be described in ways that are symbolic or contribute to the story's meaning. For example, a garden setting may evoke images of the Garden of Eden. A dry riverbed could suggest a hopeless or empty way of life. A spotless home might imply images of false perfection or sterility.

To appreciate the value and beauty of fiction, it is a good idea to read as many stories as possible in the genre that most interests you and where you hope to publish a book. All great writers are widely read and have a solid framework of understanding about the classic authors whose writings touched and changed people's lives. Grow familiar with books you love and want to emulate, and your readers can't help but fall in love with your books. Above all, look for ways to point readers to God without being overbearing or obvious:

> *"The Lord appeared from of old to me [Israel], saying, 'Yes, I have loved you with an everlasting love; therefore with loving-kindness have I drawn you and continued My faithfulness to you.'" [Deut. 7:8]*
> *—Jeremiah 31:3 AMP*

Writer's Wisdom:

How can I ensure that my book shares a Christ-centered message of hope and inspiration?

For Revelation:

"And [pray] also for me, that [freedom of] utterance may be given me, that I may open my mouth to proclaim boldly the mystery of the good news (the Gospel),"
—Ephesians 6:19 AMP

The Master's Writing Plan Activities
Step #1:

After praying for guidance, write a tentative title for your book and list the chapter titles that you want to include. While the actual titles can change later, each chapter should describe a section of the story (if fiction) or the message (if non-fiction) that the overall book will present. When you complete this activity, you should have a working book title and a list of all key points to be developed.

Step #2:

Examine each proposed chapter title to see if you can focus it even more clearly. Titles should be relatively short and need not form a complete sentence. Here are examples from a book on developing spiritual leadership:

Chapter One:	Letting Go and Letting God: Trusting God to Lead the Way
Chapter Two:	Drawing Strength from God: Get Connected via Scripture and Prayer
Chapter Three:	Finding Your Biblical Purpose

Step #3:

Compare your tentative chapter titles to make sure they don't overlap, repeat ideas, or go off in different directions. Look for interconnectedness, and yet a distinct message in each one.

New Testament Reading Plan Week #1:

Matthew 1 through Mathew 17

Chapter Two

Choose Your Topic

"The reverent and worshipful fear of the Lord
is the beginning (the chief and choice part) of Wisdom,
and the knowledge of the Holy One
Is insight and understanding."
—Proverbs 9:10 AMP

In Chapter One we discussed literary conventions that are associated with fiction and non-fiction writing. Following your companion workbook activities for Week One, you should have some thoughts written down discussing the ways in which God has inspired you to write this particular book. If you have a fairly clear notion of what you're going to write about, take a look at your paragraph summary to ensure that the topic is focused and succinct. You will need to develop a main idea, or thesis, with topical support.

At the beginning of Week Two, you are ready to dedicate your book to the Lord. You have developed a reasonable and workable writing plan, and have taken the first steps to commit your ideas to paper. Undoubtedly, you have a creative project in mind that now is taking shape, little by little, each week as you complete each chapter. Having developed a table of contents or a list of related ideas, you are crafting a fictional or non-fictional work that may influence others for many years to come.

"Who [with reason] despises the day of small things?"
—Zechariah 4:10(A) AMP

The topic is the general area of information. For example, one topic of consideration is getting teens to read the Bible. Christian parents know that guidance is important, but overbearing control is a turnoff to teens. So how should you write this book? Should it advise parents on getting teens to read the Bible? Should your book describe incentives and punishments when teens don't follow through? At this point you may be unsure. Now that you have a topic, you will want to create a thesis statement.

The thesis is the specific point or argument your book will make about the topic. Since everyone already agrees that Internet porn is bad and pervasive, you don't need to mention either of these traits in your book's thesis. Since the thesis should be narrow, arguable, and specific, you will want to start with a thesis that your book can fully develop. Possibilities include but are not limited to possibilities like the following:

1   How to get teens to read their Bible on a regular basis.
2   How to help teens develop personal devotions, or a "quiet time."
3   How parents can play a role in helping teens develop a personal relationship with God, weaning away from parents' spiritual supervision.

Possibilities like these help to narrow the focus of your intended book and prepare the author to streamline a meaningful approach that can be explored chapter by chapter. Instead of rambling about all the reasons why teens don't read their Bibles or why it's a good idea for teenagers to get into the habit of reading the Bible, the writer will limit the approach to address a problem with which readers may be struggling, using Scriptural principles for support. If you are unable to decide how to work with a general subject, try the question-and-answer approach:

1   How can I get my teenager to read the Bible more regularly?
2   What can I do to give my teen a solid spiritual foundation for reading Scripture?
3   What have I tried that hasn't worked in encouraging my teen to read the Bible? (This will help you to select a topic through the process of elimination.)

When you have narrowed the range of options for developing your topical idea, review the paragraph description you wrote for your book during the first week of this project. Look for and underline a possible thesis statement. If you don't see one, try writing one now. It may not come to you right away, but your thesis will be the next step toward moving your book through the planning stage toward development. Remember that a thesis statement (or sometimes an orienting statement) should be measurable, arguable, and logical. Don't base your book's premise on a factual claim, such as "Christian teens should read the Bible on a daily basis." Most parents will agree, and that does not make for an interesting book. You need to pray and develop a topic that will help to teach readers something they don't know or give them information they can use. The thesis should summarize in a sentence or two what the book will be about and how it will be developed.

You may have to do some free writing for several minutes to uncover hidden ideas or to create new approaches to the topic. Find a quiet corner or retreat to your office and write on paper by hand or open your word processing program on the computer screen. What most appeals to you about the idea you are considering? How can you make it pertinent to your readers who need this information? What is the message you hope to share that can change lives in positive ways? Teaching a Biblical truth in an attention-catching manner will be your primary challenge. Tell your story on paper as you would in person to a friend with the goal of bringing that person toward the light of salvation:

"This man came to witness, that he might testify of the Light, that all men might believe in it [adhere to it, trust it, and rely upon it] through him."
—John 1:7 AMP

Do Your Homework

Now that you have a general sense of your mission, it is time to take stock of what you do and don't know. You have begun by writing a summary paragraph and creating a thesis statement. The next thing you will want to do is take an inventory on the amount of information you have versus all that still is needed. Call this your "Facts List," and jot down all the basic facts you have so far about the topic.

For fiction, you may want to make this up as you go along or draw on existing notes and outlines that you plan to use for the book. For non-fiction, the list should include dates, names, and Biblical premises (principles) that you plan to write about in your book. You may not have much at this point, but at least you will know what you have to work with and what will be needed.

After completing your fact list, take some time to look it over. What appears to be missing? Start another worksheet for questions and list as many as come to mind. For non-fiction these might include the need for a definition of the problem and/or pertinent terminology. Potential reader questions can surface in issues like reliable sources to quote, statistical data, expert advice, and so on. For fiction, you may have to ask technical questions about the story's pace, timing, suspense or interest quotient, and character depth. Or you might question the story itself by asking about setting, conflicts, or plot structure.

Now you are ready to "do your homework" and find answers. If you are writing a historical romance, you can look for answers to your questions on websites devoted to the era in which your story is set to get an idea of what people wore, how they talked, what they ate, etc. For non-fiction books on the aforementioned topic of teens reading the Bible, try searching for websites that discuss the problem and what parents can do. From studies like these, you will discover a suitable niche for your book.

When researching your topic, whether fiction or non-fiction, be sure to check the most reliable Bible study materials, websites, books, and authors. The following criteria can help you select some of the more appropriate data that may be useful for your book.

1 **Date.** When was the work published? When was the website last updated? Generally speaking, it is a good idea to stick to sources not older than say, five or six years, unless you know of classic material that could be helpful.

2 **Author.** Who wrote the work? Does he or she have the Anointing plus credentials? Is the person's background appropriate for the work under consideration?

3 **Publisher.** Who published the book? Is it a commercial press known for the type of book you want to write? Is the work self-published? Who owns and/or operates the website—a junior high student or a college professor, or someone for whom the topic is an interesting but not necessarily professional duty?

4   **Is the information reliable?** This will depend in part on the publisher and the author, but also on the statistical data used for support.

5   **Are there copyright limitations to your using the material?** Some writing is in the public domain and may be freely referenced. Many authors do not mind your quoting a few sentences from their work as long as you attribute it to them and make wise use of their material so that no embarrassments or conflict of interest ensue.

Double-check Your Sources

If you plan to quote or borrow material from other sources, be prepared to cite it correctly in your non-fiction book or attribute it appropriately in your novel or story. Depending on the type of book you are writing, you can choose from many styles of documentation. Among the most popular are the Modern Language Association (MLA) and Chicago Manual of Style (CMS) for in-text citations and endnotes as well as bibliographies. There are other style guides to choose from as well, so select the one that is typically used with this style of writing. For some books, no experts or outside sources will be quoted, so you don't have to worry about technical citations.

If you do quote a source, double-check to make sure you have cited it word-for-word if you have placed the quote between double quotations marks. Paraphrases and summaries can be described in your own words, but you still have to give credit to the original source by using an in-text citation or endnote. A bibliography, or "Works Cited" page, will be placed at the end of the story according to your publisher's discretion to give credit where needed.

After browsing websites and reading articles or the Bible about your topic, start taking notes (citing page numbers for quotes and paraphrases) so you will become more informed on the topic and about your book's potential niche. This will give you a better idea of how to prepare your thesis and table of contents as you begin shaping the message. You will start to feel and sound like an expert on the subject.

Establish a Framework

After crafting your book's message in a thesis, creating a facts list, and then researching online and print sources to supplement your knowledge base, your next step will be to develop a series of points that each expand on part of the thesis. Most books have several chapters that are numbered or that use headings. This will help you divide your topic into workable sections. The old divide-and-conquer strategy works well when applied to a writing project of this size.

You may want to use an outline, not necessarily the old fashioned kind learned in middle school with its Roman numerals and capital letters. You can simply list sub-points drawn from the thesis idea, and then below each sup-point, add several details or examples that you can use to write about that point that will help readers to grasp and appreciate it. The outline is a tentative step in creating a skeleton for your book's idea. This framework will help you expand the central idea into specific areas that need to be explored and discussed for the reader's benefit.

When you have a topic, thesis, and outline, this is a good time to brainstorm the particulars of the book you want to write. Brainstorming means taking some time to think about the direction you want the book to go. For fiction, this could entail several options as you think about plot, characters, setting, and other elements. For non-fiction, brainstorming helps you take a problem-solving approach to decide what to offer readers in your book.

> *"For the rest, brethren, whatever is true, whatever is worthy of reverence and is honorable and seemly, whatever is just, whatever is pure, whatever is lovely and lovable, whatever is kind and winsome and gracious, if there is any virtue and excellence, if there is anything worthy of praise, think on and weigh and take account of these things [fix your minds on them]."*
> *—Philippians 4:8-9 AMP*

After writing an outline, set it aside for a day or two. Give yourself time to think about what you wrote and whether that is truly the direction you want the book to go. Then return to your outline, read it over, and edit it to make changes you have decided are necessary.

You may need to review your material intermittently over several days time to clarify the message you want to send readers. Don't worry about editing or polishing right now. This is the time to get your focus in place, along with a basic outline of information that will be offered throughout each chapter. You will correct and polish your writing work toward the end of our twelve-week session.

* * *

The practical aspects of writing—thinking of ideas, deciding how to describe them, and considering a reader's need for information—may seem to draw the focus away from closeness with God. But the truth is that the two go hand in hand. Foremost is the need to be grounded in God's Word on a daily basis. When you read, study, reflect on, and pray over a Scriptural passage each day, and then think about ways you can apply it to your life and writing, you provide God a conduit through which to channel His Spirit. Pray over each segment of your book, asking God questions in prayer and waiting for His answers in that still, small voice. Later, you will seek feedback from Godly mentors and responsible readers that can help to shape your book for an audience of readers:

"If indeed God permits, we will [now] proceed [to advanced teaching]."
—Hebrews 6:3 AMP

There may be times over this 90-day period when you will feel like giving up. Or you may slow down and feel unsure about which way to go. Such feelings are natural. Some may occur for good reason—like pressing job duties or family needs. But if you find yourself in pursuit of elusive creativity, you cannot afford to put your book on hold. The secret to prolific writing is to keep writing! The more you write on a regular basis, whether you feel like it or not, the easier it will be to continue doing so. In fact, studies show that the physical actions of writing or typing can stimulate the neurons in your brain to produce ideas and move your writing along. Don't give up! Don't stop! That's part of the 90-day system. Keep writing even when you are not completely sure of your message or the value of your ideas. When you have completed the chapter for that week, then go back and re-read it to see how it sounds. You can then rewrite some parts that need attention. Later chapters of this book will provide time for review and editing, too.

Now you are ready to begin developing the substance of your book. Look over the summary, thesis, outline, and questions, along with a list of experts or outside source information, to be sure you have everything you need to get started. Armed with a solid idea, support information, and an outline of subtopics, you can start crafting a book that will be ready to market in twelve weeks.

> *"A [self-confident] fool has no delight in understanding but only*
> *in revealing his personal opinions and himself."*
> *—Proverbs 18:2 AMP*

Be sure to take time to thank God for His inspiration and this opportunity. Read and meditate on the Scripture below. Then go to your accompanying companion workbook and answer the questions for Week One. Then write a rough draft of your introductory ideas to get the ball rolling, and—you're on your way at last, so that you can share in the Apostle John's mission to God's people:

> *"And we are now writing these things to you so that our joy [in seeing*
> *you included] may be full [and your joy may be complete]."*
> *—I John 1:4 AMP*

* * *

Writer's Wisdom:
How can I use my writing to inspire others in the Christian faith?

For Revelation:
> *"Then He [thoroughly] opened up their minds to understand the*
> *Scriptures,"*
> *—Luke 24:45 AMP*

The Master's Writing Plan Activities
Writing Step #1:
Write a short paragraph that describes your book's mission. Then go back to your list of chapter headings and write a sentence or two describing what each chapter will be about.

Writing Step #2:

Compare your book's mission paragraph to the short descriptions for each chapter. Explain in another sentence added to each chapter description how each chapter is linked to, and will help develop, your book's mission as described in the preliminary paragraph.

Writing Step #3:

Study your book's chapter descriptions and the added sentences that show how the chapters will develop the book's purpose (in the mission paragraph). Then list at least two or three points to be included for development in each chapter. These points will fulfill your book's purpose by discussing information in the chapter that will inform and guide readers' understanding of your topic. Here are examples from a book on how parents can continue to spiritually influence adult (grown) children:

Mission:

This book will provide readers with information about how parents can still impact adult children for the Lord by following specific, helpful strategies that will preserve the parent-child relationship while guiding spiritual influence in certain contexts.

Chapter One: Let Go and Let God.

This chapter explains how parents must release their children as they reach adulthood, transferring the care and guidance of mature offspring to God. Yet parents continue to have a spiritual influence in a variety of ways. One is by demonstrating that parents are trusting God for the son or daughter's future, and that moms and dads still hope to play a positive guiding role when young adults need advice, admonishment, or comfort.

New Testament Reading Plan Week #2:

Matthew 18 through Mark 3

Chapter Three

Consider Your Audience

"Write therefore the things you see,
what they are [and signify]
and what is to take place hereafter."
—*Revelation 1:19 AMP*

God knew exactly who His intended readership for the Bible would be—He created us! Despite our free will and human imperfections, God made consistent efforts to communicate with us from the time of creation to the present day. First, He spent time with Adam in the Garden of Eden, talking directly to the man He had formed from the dust. But when the first couple sinned by eating forbidden fruit, God distanced Himself from them by evicting the pair from the Garden of Eden and placing an angel there to guard the entrance so they could never again enjoy its fruits and beauty.

> *"Therefore the Lord God sent him forth from the Garden of Eden to till the ground from which he was taken.*
> *So [God] drove out the man; and He placed at the east of the Garden of Eden the cherubim and a flaming sword which turned every way, to keep and guard the way to the tree of life. [Rev. 2:7, 22:2, 14, 19.]"*
> —*Genesis 3:23-24 AMP*

Would God have spoken directly to all His offspring? We don't know. Later, as more people populated the earth, it seems that God spoke only to those who earned His favor, like Noah, Abraham, and Moses, the men who became leaders that would forge a new nation of people set apart as sanctified to God—the Jews, who would inherit the land of Israel.

From the time the Israelites were released from slavery in Egypt, God gave His chosen people the Ten Commandments through Moses on Mount Sinai. Later, the Levite priests wrote interpretations, expansions, and laws from the Commandments, which served as another kind of writing to guide Jewish worship and lifestyles. This testimony was directed by Moses, and later through the prophets, who wrote their own records that helped to direct Israel's rulers and priests. God no longer spoke directly with His people; He gave them written commands through the few individuals whom He entrusted:

> *"Moses wrote all the words of the Lord. He rose up early in the morning and built an altar at the foot of the mountain and set up twelve pillars representing Israel's twelve tribes."*
> *—Exodus 24:4 AMP*

Following ages of prophecy and later, the Babylonian exile, the Jews settled into a painful period of silence—about 400 years, when God did not speak to them at all. Lonely and bewildered, longing for spiritual fellowship with their Creator, the Jews waited for the Promised One who would become their intermediary and a direct link between God and humans. Eventually, Jesus was born as the promised Messiah. Once more, God spoke directly to His people through His Son. But not everyone was listening. Somehow God ordained that the Gospels would be recorded for successive generations. So Jesus' followers wrote of His words and deeds, capturing for all time the essence of God's plan of salvation to everyone who believes and accepts it:

> *"It seemed good and desirable to me, [and so I have determined] also after having searched out diligently and followed all things closely and traced accurately the course from the highest to the minutest detail from the very first, to write an orderly account for you, most excellent Theophilus [Acts 1:1.]."*
> *—Luke 1:3 AMP*

Later, the Apostle Paul was converted to Christianity on the road to Damascus—this time God used sign language, as He had with the Old Testament prophet Balaam. It worked! Saul became Paul and embarked on an evangelistic ministry to the Gentiles:

> *"[But] to this day I have had the help which comes from God [as*
> *my ally], and so I stand here testifying to small and great alike,*
> *asserting nothing beyond what the prophets and Moses declared*
> *would come to pass—"*
> *—Acts 26:22 AMP*

Establishing churches in key regions throughout Europe and Asia Minor, Paul subsequently wrote letters to encourage new converts and church builders in holding fast to the original Christian doctrines and refraining from worldly or sinful behavior. His letters, along with the written testimonies of the disciples, help to comprise the most important writing that has ever been known to us—the Holy Bible, breathed out as divine inspiration to save, teach, and guide Christians throughout time:

> *"For I am not ashamed of the Gospel (good news) of Christ, for*
> *it is God's power working unto salvation [for deliverance from*
> *eternal death] to everyone who believes with a personal trust and*
> *a confident surrender and firm reliance, to the Jew first and also*
> *to the Greek"*
> *—Romans 1:16 AMP*

God knew His audience well—He created us, after all. He knew what it would take to get people to heed His words and follow His advice. We all fall short, and some do not listen at all, but through pre-ordained prophets, apostles, kings, and priests, God's Word has been preserved through the ages for those who have been designated hearers. God used many instruments through which to channel His voice to those who would listen:

1   Prophets
2   Priests
3   Kings
4   Disciples
5   Apostles

These men and women have written praise, warnings, complaints, fears, advice, and instructions to the intended readers of their message. As the most widely read book in the world ever known, the Bible's collection of writing styles and messages makes it unique among the classic works written by people through the ages.

As human writers partaking of a divine message and ministry, we do not have the luxury of knowing in advance who will read our book. All we know is we've been given a mission and the skills to accomplish it with the help of the Holy Spirit. But as you develop your book's concepts and write them in a skillful, attention-grabbing way, you will need an idea of who might be reading the published book somewhere down the road and how it might impact them for Christ. You might be able to assume the following to a certain degree about many of your potential readers:

1   They are literate. They can read, or someone can read the book to them.
2   They are curious about Christianity. Perhaps they've heard or read something about it elsewhere.
3   They may be able to learn from your book's message, so prepare it prayerfully.
4   They may compare your ideas to those of other writers.
5   The Holy Spirit may use your book to convict them of their need for salvation.

Think of God preparing the Ten Commandments for His chosen people while they wandered in a hot, desolate wilderness in search of a country and an identity. God wrote the Commandments on tablets of stone, intending them to last. They weren't written in the dust or on parchment, which would crumble. Nor were they entrusted to the priests for memorization as a way of sharing them with the populace. The fact of their permanence means He wanted more than just the Israelites under Moses' leadership to read, learn, and remember them. The Israelites accepted God's Word as divine guidance for their lives individually and collectively. Transcending time, place, and identity features like race and gender, the Commandments inspired awe in readers, and they continue to hold clear and special meaning for God's followers today. The Ten Commandments were given to Moses as spiritual guidance for the Israelites who were forging a new racial and religious identity that would culminate in their settling in the

Promised Land, Israel. To make the Ten Commandments understandable and binding to the Israelites and their descendents for thousands of years to come, God wrote His Laws clearly. His pronouncements are numbered, they are prioritized, and they are distinct from one another. All Christian messages should follow God's unique and powerful style to convey spiritual messages in today's world:

> *"And Moses turned and went down from the mountain with the two tables of the Testimony in his hand, tables or tablets that were written on both sides.*
>
> *The tables were the work of God; the writing was the writing of God, graven upon the tables."*
>
> *—Exodus 32:15-16 AMP*
>
> *"The LORD said to Moses, Cut two tables of stone like the first, and I will write upon these tables the words that were on the first tables, which you broke."*
>
> *—Exodus 34:1 AMP*
>
> *"For we write you nothing else but simply what you can read and understand [there is no double meaning to what we say], and I hope that you will become thoroughly acquainted [with divine things] and know and understand [them] accurately and well to the end"*
>
> *—2 Corinthians 1:13 AMP*

Moses was the messenger. God entrusted him with receiving and transmitting divine law to human subjects. We might think of Moses as the publisher. In this case, though, there was no need to edit or proofread the work; it was perfect. Moses' main duty was to promote or market the Ten Commandments. He did this effectively by following God's leading with building the tabernacle and leading the people to selected destinations. As judge and overseer of the Israelites, Moses must have had many occasions to draw people's attentions to God's mandates for human behavior. Today, many in our culture still follow the Ten Commandments and attempt to make them part of our spiritual leadership and legal jurisprudence. Sadly, some have blocked the latter effort, choosing to place man's law above God's given ordinances. Still, God's awesome message has lasted thousands of years and remains in full force today. God knew His audience,

He had a clear sense of purpose for His message, and He chose a reliable messenger:

> *"Then does He Who supplies you with His marvelous [Holy] Spirit and works powerfully and miraculously among you do so on [the grounds of your doing] what the Law demands, or because of your believing in and adhering to and trusting in and relying on the message that you heard?"*
> —*Galatians 3:5 AMP*

Try to envision an audience for your book. In your mind's eye, can you see what your readers look like? How old are they? Are they mostly male or female, or is it a mixed group? What are their interests? How much education do they have? What type of relationship with God do they enjoy? What can your book do to help them grow spiritually?

> *"Now Faith is the assurance (the confirmation, the title deed) of the things [we] hope for, being the proof of things [we] do not see and the conviction of their reality [faith perceiving as real fact what is not revealed to the senses]."*
> —*Hebrews 11:1 AMP*

These are some of the questions an author must consider when writing for a Christian audience. While you may not be able to visualize exactly who will pick up your book from a shelf or order it online, you must have some idea of your target audience. If you're writing a romance novel, then you can expect more female than male readers, probably in all age brackets, but predominantly in their twenties and thirties. But if you are developing a non-fiction book on Christians and politics, you probably will attract more male than female readers, many or most with college educations and holding professional or middle-class jobs. These are all generalities, but they give you an idea of readership demographics. You can learn more by visiting publishing websites that provide information about what people are reading these days.

Most books cannot be written to satisfy readers of all ages. Rather, they are intended to grab the interests of a certain age group, such as children, teens, women or men 25-44, seniors, and so on. You will want to think about the type of person who is likely to find your book interesting. At this point, you might not be sure. It's okay to continue writing your book as you contemplate the reader group that will get the most from your topic and style. In the meantime, here are some reader characteristics to keep in mind while writing your book:

1. Age.
2. Education.
3. Gender.
4. Marital status.
5. Occupation or profession.
6. Socio-economic background.
7. Spiritual condition (saved vs. unsaved).
8. Interest level in Christianity.
9. Interest level in your book's topic.
10. Reading ability/fluency.

While all your readers are unlikely to share every characteristic in this list, it may be helpful to focus your book toward a certain group of readers. For example, men between the ages of 18 and 60 might enjoy a book that describes how an adventurous or playboy lifestyle brought the author closer to God. On the other hand, women between the ages of 30 and 50 could appreciate a book on parenting daughters in the area of relationships. It is possible, naturally, and even desirable those readers from other groups might find these books interesting, but having a target audience will help you write in a specific manner that will grab and hold the attention of at least that group of readers.

In writing your book, you will want to shape the language, style, and tone according to your readers' interests. For example, we talk to children one way, teens another, professionals in a different style, and older adults in yet another. Sometimes we address men and women differently, or college educated people from those with a high school diploma. The genre, or type of writing, that you pursue also makes a difference in the way your message comes across to those who are reading it.

"For He was teaching as One Who had [and was] authority, and not as [did] the scribes."
—Matthew 7:29 AMP

Vocabulary and dialogue play an important role in writing. The type of language expressed in your book can either help readers to understand and appreciate the ideas behind the writing, or it can confuse or bore them. In fiction, dialogue should sound realistic for the time period represented. Some writers try to bring Bible stories up to date by letting the characters speak as we do in modern times. That may work in certain books, as long as it doesn't sound artificial or make the characters seem phony.

The tone of a book creates a mood that can influence readers. For example, if you write a book calling readers' attention to a social crisis in our country, you may infuse a tone (or mood) of outrage, alarm, or sorrow, depending on the point behind your writing and how you want readers to react. In an adventure novel, you may want to create a mood of suspense, which will be important for grabbing the readers' attention and keeping them turning the pages. An author has influence over his or her readership in evoking certain moods that will incite them to adopt new views or take personal action.

Development includes detail, examples, illustrations, and/or evidence. In developing your book, you are providing the support for your ideas that will make the book convincing and interesting to your readership. For example, you can claim that a certain lifestyle is wrong, but the general population endorses it, you will need to do research and cite facts to show that your concern is merited. You could decide to take a Bible-only approach, but this means you will need to know and research the Bible thoroughly and use a widely-accepted version for citations. Or, if you take the approach of including social research, for example, on the subject of teen pregnancy, you need to know which research is reliable and will be acceptable to your readers. Make sure of your own beliefs before you try to convince others of them in your book. This must be done in a way that will not only let you express your Christian views, but also provide facts, statistics, and Biblical examples to convince readers of their validity.

Considerations like these can help your book to be successful. Although you may want to attract readers of every age and background, chances are your book will be of primary interest to a special group composed of certain types of readers. Typically, a book should fit into a specific market niche. An author needs to have a vision about where the book will be sold and who will buy it. You might think to yourself, "My book is a cross between *The Purpose Driven Life* and *Reposition Yourself.*" Assuming a publisher is familiar with the two works you reference, he will get a fair idea of how to market your book upon publication.

> *"And the Lord answered me and said, Write the vision and engrave it so plainly upon tablets that everyone who passes may [be able to] read [it easily and quickly] as he hastens by.*
> *For the vision is yet for an appointed time and it hastens to the end [fulfillment]: it will not deceive or disappoint. Though it tarry, wait [earnestly] for it, because it will surely come: it will not be behindhand on its appointed day. [Heb. 10:37, 38.]"*
> *—Habakkuk 2:2-3 AMP*

Authors who self-publish their books need to understand the book market even better. Most self-published books have a limited budget for marketing, and that amount must be used to focus on a group of customers who have the best chance of getting interested in your book. There's no point in paying thousands of dollars to mail a flier describing your publication on raising teens in a postmodern world to senior citizens whose kids are already grown. Granted, they may be interested in the book for their children to read in raising the grandkids, but you probably would attract more buyers by aiming publicity at parents of teenagers. Marketing dollars, which can be limited, should be used for the best possible results.

Readers want to know what to expect when they purchase your book. Typically, a buyer spends six seconds reading the front or back cover before making a purchasing decision. The cover blurb needs to clearly state what the book is about and what it will do for readers. This book's title says it all: Write your book in 90 days, doing it God's way. Your book should fit into a certain category of publications so that fans of that category will know what they're getting when they pick up your book while browsing. In fact, a newly published book will not be placed on a store bookshelf until the manager knows what type of book it is and how to market it. Bookstore managers don't have time to figure out where to place a book of an uncertain genre. While it's true that some books are crossbred between two or more niches, such volumes are rare and they sometimes sell poorly. With a first book especially, it is wise to be cautious and get your book to blend in with others, not stand out as an anomaly.

Who Will Want to Read Your Book?

Attracting a reading audience depends on whom you are writing for. If you are working on a mystery novel, then mystery novel lovers are your target audience. If you are preparing a biography of E. W. Kenyon, then you will be writing for people who enjoy reading Christian biographies or books on contemporary spiritual leaders.

To understand more about your audience needs, it is important to learn something about the genre that your book will join. Remember that various writing forms in the Bible follow conventions of their day. Letters (epistles) began with the signature first, as opposed to the style today in which letters close with the signature. The books of history are similar to other historical accounts of their respective eras. If you want to write a Christian historical romance, you had better learn something about Christian historical romances. If you are writing a Christian thriller, read a few Christian thrillers. You also might decide to read non-Christian work only because it has proven successful and has set the standard form and structure for publishers, bookstores, and buyers. Obviously, your characters, plot, and action will assume Christian characteristics and reveal a spiritual message.

You don't have to assume that only Christians will be interested in your book. Depending on the topic and the skillfulness of your writing style, you may be able to attract non-Christian readers who want to know more about your ideas or who admire the way you write. They could decide to check out your book based on a word-of-mouth recommendation from a friend or family member. Or, when browsing a bookstore or library shelf, or perhaps reading a review about your publication, a reader might be tempted to give it a try, even if the genre, author, or theme is different from his or her usual reading fare.

Libraries, gift shops, and bookstores may be interested in stocking copies if the topic is relevant and there is an established fan base because of your website blog or serial excerpts, or due to the genre or topic. Plan to write your book in a balanced way that will appeal to a select group of intended readers without shutting out other inquisitive souls who pick up a copy and might decide to read it. Most likely you will have friends, coworkers, neighbors, and relatives who will buy a copy, so be mindful not to print anything that could be offensive or embarrassing to people you know. Clearly, Christians shouldn't write offensive material in any case, but we all know of super-sensitive people that could be hurt or upset by reading about themselves in print, even if it's just a warm-hearted anecdote or snippet of dialogue. Visit www.writeitGodsway.com for details on additional writing and marketing tools.

Non-Fiction Genres

Self-help books generally sell well when they are marketed well. These books offer help, guidance, or insight for positive living. They should include expert credentials, like a college degree, job experience, or research support. Some are based on personal experience, like a healthy way to lose fifty pounds or balancing work with family duties. Christian themes might include becoming a Godlier parent, getting along with non-Christian coworkers, surviving a relationship loss (parent, child, sibling, and spouse), building an effective Christian testimony in your community, and so on.

Books on spiritual living or Biblical principles also attract many buyers. This type of writing helps less mature believers (or even non-believers) to understand Christian behavior or faith-building strategies.

Christian histories or biographies enjoy a place of note on publishers' lists, but they do not often sell as widely as other kinds of Christian books. Based on real events or people, this style of writing must be factual and supported by accurate research that often includes interviews with the subject person and possible family members or friends.

Devotionals and Bible studies offer support for individuals or groups who want to study the Bible or improve their spiritual lives. These books rely heavily on Biblical references and scholarly interpretations as support for readers.

Fiction Genres

Action/adventure books are built on a plot involving conflict and/or competition, like trying to survive a snowstorm while stranded in the forest, or training to compete in a sport against a long-time champion. Readers love cheering for a hero, and they enjoy seeing the good guy win. When the villain succeeds, however, the story is considered a tragedy.

Suspense/thriller books are similar to action/adventures, but they have a stronger plot with more at stake. These can be cops-and-robber stories or a crisis based on secular or supernatural events.

Romance novels take many forms, including historical, contemporary, urban, Gothic, and others. With happy endings that typically unify a couple whose relationship has been shrouded in uncertainty, these books make great escape reading, with a readership comprising young women in particular.

The above are not the only type of books in today's Christian publishing market, but they are representative of the more common kind and the best sellers. Think of *The Purpose-Driven Life* as an example of non-fiction and the *Left Behind* series representing fiction for examples of popular books in the Christian market.

Book Elements

As discussed in Chapter One, fiction and non-fiction genres include books that are structured with an introduction, several topical chapters of development, and a conclusion. In other words, you will want to lead into your message, deliver it, and then bow out gracefully while leaving readers with a summary or final point to ponder.

The flow of fiction needs to move the story forward. You will want to try and balance the pace of each chapter in a relatively even way. Certain areas of the story, like the midpoint and finale, can move faster, but overall, the plot should move rapidly enough to keep readers' attention and slow enough to engage their interest. The narrator should seem believable or at least compelling. Some stories even have a plural narrator, like the townspeople ("we") in William Faulkner's short story, "A Rose for Emily."

Fictional books can take several forms, some of which may seem to be drawn from real life, but are actually embellishments or complete fabrications of events:

1 Biography of a fictional person, like a story about the last Civil War veteran
2 Drama based on real events, like Arthur Miller's *The Crucible*
3 Journal entries as a way of revealing a character's thoughts or struggles
4 A memoir comprising a mixture of true and untrue information (thus, fiction)
5 Stories told from more than one character's perspective in interspersed chapters

6   Expose revealing alleged crimes, cover-ups, or personal actions of
     characters

7   A purported history of a family or town

If you think about stories in the Bible, you can appreciate the value
of differing modes. The story of Adam and Eve in the Garden of Eden is
revealed by narrated actions, the characters are memorable and realistic,
the tone is objective and yet suspenseful, the narrator is all-knowing and
accurate—all of these features make a real event interesting and meaningful. With a unique setting and universal symbols, this opening chapter
in the saga of human life creates dramatic tension that draws and informs
readers. As you read other accounts in the Bible, you will find many of
these same elements, along with others. God is the master Storyteller,
although all of His stories are true and purposeful.

Non-fiction elements include a main point. The narrator might use
third person, for example, "People who read the Bible regularly are happier
than those who don't." But a personal narrator may use first person voice:
"My studies have revealed that regular Bible readers are happy people."
Diction style is important. Using informal diction and casual speech make
a book seem personal and accessible. But the down side to this style is that
it may not seem serious enough, especially if the topic is critical. Formal
diction is usually reserved for government documents and scholarly writings. Slang is used mainly in novels to show how certain characters speak.
Most non-fiction writers do not use much slang, which can make the book
seem unprofessional.

It isn't difficult to match your writing to a genre and give it the elements
needed for the book to be successful. All authors should write for a target
audience while developing their books, just as God had us in mind while
revealing the Word to us through the Bible.

Writer's Wisdom:
How should I shape my book for those who need to hear about
Jesus?

For Revelation:
*"And He said, He who has ears to hear, let him be hearing [and
let him consider, and comprehend]." Mark 4:9 AMP*

The Master's Writing Plan Activities
Writing Step #1:

Now that you have a sense of purpose for your book, start browsing useful Web resources, Christian books and articles, and possibly videotapes or seminar notes (if you have attended any related to your book's topic). Organize these by chapter topic and keep them separate for easy reference when you begin writing each chapter.

Writing Step #2:

Take good notes on your research, carefully citing the authors, names of works, and publication information for each source you plan to cite in your book. Review your notes to decide which sources you will keep, and which, to discard. If you still need more research, continue reading and searching for the most relevant and up-to-date material.

Writing Step #3:

Begin writing a rough draft of the first chapter, using research to support your ideas or to provide helpful support, such as statistics, case studies, or examples from real life (interviews, books, etc.). Choose a documentation style in which to cite your book's references, such as the Chicago Manual of Style (CMS), often used by journalists and non-fiction writers, which you can buy at the store or check online at http://www.chicagomanualofstyle.org/home.html.

When referencing research from print or online sources, you need to cite sources properly by following documentation style guidelines.

New Testament Reading Plan Week #3:

Mark 4 to Mark 16

Chapter Four

Let the Word Be Heard:

Self-Publishing vs. Commercial Publishing

"And He said to them, 'Is the lamp brought in to be put under
a peck measure or under a bed,
and not [to be put] on the lampstand?'"
—Mark 4:21

N̲ow that you have begun writing your book based on The Master's Writing Plan activities in Chapters One through Three, it's time to start thinking about how you will get your message into the hands of your target market. Previously we discussed the need to narrow your marketing focus to a certain segment of readers who will appreciate your type of book as well as benefit from it. So we have a writer—you; a message—your book; and readers—your audience. Your book needs to be geared to the type of readers who will take note and benefit:

"For whoever finds me [Wisdom] finds life and draws forth and
obtains favor from the Lord."
—Proverbs 8:35 AMP

Now you need to choose the most effective vehicle for delivering your message to selected readers. Factors to keep in mind will include timeliness, cost, and packaging. But keep in mind that whichever method of distribution seems best suited to your book, no matter how difficult it may be, God can help you make use of the vehicle if it is His will. Your goal is to deliver a valuable and insightful message to help others find God or enhance their walk with Him:

> *"The [consistently] righteous man is a guide to his neighbor, but the way of the wicked causes others to go astray."*
> *—Proverbs 12:26 AMP*

God always chooses the best carriers for His communications with us. On important occasions, He has spoken to men and women directly, as evidenced in Genesis 3 where God addresses Adam and Eve following their disobedience. God also conveyed critical information through trusted messengers like Abraham, to whom He foretold the destruction of Sodom and Gomorrah and to leaders like Moses, to whom was relayed the Ten Commandments. Throughout the Old Testament God appointed prophets, rulers, and leaders to carry His words to those who would listen. Sometimes, as with Isaiah, these messengers knew their mission would accomplish little good. Still, they were bound to deliver it and pray for Godly outcomes. God's people have no choice but to obey His Will and try to influence the world to believe and turn to God Almighty:

> *"Also I heard the voice of the Lord, saying, 'Whom shall I send? And who will go for Us?' Then said I, 'Here am I; send me.'*
> *And He said, 'Go and tell this people, 'Hear and hear continually, but understand not; and see and see continually, but do not apprehend with your mind.*
> *Make the heart of this people fat; and make their ears heavy and shut their eyes, lest they see with their eyes and hear with their ears and understand with their hearts and turn again and be healed.'*
> *'Then said I, 'Lord, how long?' And He answered, 'Until cities lie waste without inhabitant and houses without man, and the land is utterly desolate.*
> *And the Lord removes [His] people far away, and the forsaken places are many in the midst of the land.*
> *And though a tenth [of the people] remain in the land, it will be for their destruction [eaten up and burned] like a terebinth tree*

or like an oak whose stump and substance remain when they are felled or have cast their leaves. The holy seed [the elect remnant] is the stump and substance [of Israel].'"
—Isaiah 6:8-13 AMP

At other times, however, God chose different instruments to deliver His words, like the Angel that revealed the future to Daniel. Handwriting on the wall, dew on fleeces, and the "small, still voice" are more ways in which God interacted with the people He selected to receive special messages. Today our Heavenly Father primarily communicates with believers via prayer and Scripture as well as through ministers and circumstances. God knows how to get our attention to tell us important things—if we are willing to listen!

"Let all those that seek and require You rejoice and be glad in You; let such as love Your salvation say continually, 'The Lord be magnified!'"
—Psalm 40:16 AMP

Similarly, writers throughout history have found various ways to impact others with their thoughts and words. The oral tradition involved memorizing and reciting key facts of a culture through storytelling or singing. Many scholars believe that parts of the Old Testament, especially the family lineages, were memorized and recited in this fashion to preserve them in an era when most people were illiterate and lacked basic reading and writing skills. Nowadays, most of us can think of older relatives who repeat their favorite stories from military duty, farm labor, or family dramas over and over, which is their way of preserving a legacy. God's Word encourages us to share the Gospel with others:

"And [pray] also for me, that [freedom of] utterance may be given me, that I may open my mouth to proclaim boldly the mystery of the good news (the Gospel)"
—Ephesians 6:19 AMP

The written word emerged from civilizations that had alphabetic, phonetic, pictorial or other codes by which to encapsulate ideas for others to read. Scraps of parchment, inscribed architecture, and imprinted scrolls preceded the development of today's paper and ink or keyboard. Whether you write by hand or on the computer, you can have a printable document. Words on pages are the main medium today to communicate with others and share vital information.

Depending on the purpose behind your writing, you will want to think about publishing possibilities. If you are organizing a book of sermons, for example, you may want to use desktop publishing options to organize an attractive, readable collection of topics for others to use in Bible studies or personal devotions. Perhaps your sermons will be bound for church use. Or you may decide to tie them together in a common theme and publish the collection as a book for readers outside your church membership to read. Whatever you are writing, give it your best effort:

> *"Whatever may be your task, work at it heartily (from the soul), as [something done] for the Lord and not for men"*
> *—Colossians 3:23 AMP*

Other authors may prefer to search for a commercial publisher, one that will pay a handsome advance as well as generous royalties based on the number of copies that a book sells. But finding a publisher and reaping fruitful rewards may take more time and energy than many authors care to invest. More and more these days, publishing companies expect authors to contribute to marketing their books to the public by arranging book-signings in their local area, writing articles for publication, and giving talks to civic organizations. Many authors prefer not to take a public role regarding their books, but rather to write behind the scenes. This is an important point to work out with a publisher before signing a contract.

On the other hand, a publishing company handles all of the business of selling your book, such as developing marketing materials, tracking sales and returns, and calculating royalty payments. This can be an attractive option for writers who do not care for the bookkeeping aspects of publishing their work, along with record-keeping of your writing schedule and tax preparation.

While a commercial publisher may seem like a logical choice, consider these facts from Parapublishing.com and Book Statistics http:// BookStatistics.com:

1 In 2004 there were 85,000 book publishers. About 11,000 publishers purchased new ISBNs. —PWDaily http://www.publishersweekly. com/PWdaily/CA510344.html

2 Publisher statistics:
   —6 large publishers (in New York)
   —3-400 medium-sized publishers
   —86,000 small/self-publishers

1 The six U.S. conglomerate publishers:
   2 Random House, Inc.
   3 Penguin Putnam Inc.
   4 HarperCollins
   5 Holtzbrinck Publishing Holdings
   6 Time Warner
   7 Simon & Schuster, Inc.

7 In 2006 U.S. title output in 2006 increased by more than 3% to 291,920 new titles and editions, up from the 282,500 published in 2005 http://www.bowker.com/press/bowker/2007_0531_bowker. htm

8 Commercial publishers may or may not pay an advance against future book earnings, and royalties are paid just once or twice a year, on average (see the current issue of *Writer's Market* for individual publisher listings).

9 The author's actual rate of return on his or her book typically runs between five and twelve percent. So if your book sells for $15 a copy, you could receive between $.75 and $1.80 per copy.

10 If you receive an advance, and your book doesn't sell enough copies to "pay back" the advance to the publisher, you may have a hard time getting another book contract.

11 Publishers don't spend as much time as they used to promoting your book. Many authors help to promote the book in hopes of making greater sales, which can take away time and effort from the writing process and the next book.

12 A publishing contract should be clearly reviewed before signing, preferably with the help of an intellectual property attorney (or one

with experience in the publishing field). Failure to effectively nego-tiate the contract could result in an author's decreased revenues and loss of rights. Points to consider include any advances to be paid, copying costs, permission requests (for researched material), number of copies for the first run, film rights (if applicable), foreign rights, audio book options, and collateral materials (mugs, t-shirts, etc.).

If you are considering self-publishing, you will retain greater control over your publishing venture and rights, but you also will carry greater responsibility for printing, marketing, and shipping it, unless you hire experts to handle these duties for you. Here are a few things to keep in mind:

1 The author retains control of the book's publication and marketing plan.
2 Self-published authors can expect to earn royalties near or beyond 50%.
3 While authors still spend considerable time promoting their books, they receive a greater percentage of profits and may enjoy enhanced reader relations that will establish a fan base for future books and products.
4 Self-publishing success depends largely on the author's initiative and creativity in getting the book into the right readers' hands. Visit www.writeitGodsway.com for marketing tips.

Consult Self-publishing References

God self-published the Bible, and it has remained a best seller for thousands of years. Although originally published in part as the Old Testament, those Books of the Bible remained very important to the kings of Israel and Judah, as well as to the faithful Israelite followers who loved and served God. Later, the New Testament was "published" in sections comprising the Gospels, the Apostles' letters, and John's prophetic vision of Revelation. By the mid-16th century, a complete Bible was available in English, although the authorized King James Version did not appear until 1611. See "English Bible History" at www.greatsite.com/timeline-english-bible-history for more information. Since then, the entire Bible as we know it today has continued to inspire awe in readers and convert unbelievers.

When you are ready to start promoting your book and schedule book signings, the first step will be to create a media kit that includes several if not all of the following items:

1 Press release
2 The galley or pre-published book
3 Author bio
4 Photo (head shot)
5 Business card
6 One sheet
7 Reviews of your book
8 Speaking topics and previous presentations
9 List of author's articles on the same or related topic
10 Copies of newspaper articles and interviews about the book or author
11 Promotional items (bookmarks, pens)

In addition to sending your media packet to newspapers, magazines, websites, radio stations, and TV stations, gear your efforts to special groups like the following:

1 National Religious Broadcasters (NRB) (www.nrb.org)
2 Christian Book Association (CBA) (www.cbaonline.org)
3 Church Libraries (www.eclalibraries.org/magazine.htm)

You should start announcing your book's publication several months before it is printed as a "heads up" to your target audience. Building readers' interest can help to create a market niche for the book so they will be watching for the print volume when it finally appears on bookshelves or online. Fan your readers' interest so they will be ready to pick up copies when the book is finally released to the public.

Speaking Presentations
While writing your book, as you become an expert on specific and related topics, you can start promoting yourself as a public speaker to draw attention to the book so you will have a ready audience following its publication. You will need to develop a select number of topics drawn from your research for the book, as well as any related subjects or news items. Always check news headlines and keep holidays as well as seasons and special

dates in mind to tie your book in and make it relevant. For example, a book about former President Jimmy Carter's spiritual legacy might draw public interest around Presidents Day in February, while a devotional based on "an attitude of gratitude" could enjoy heightened attention at Thanksgiving.

Prepare a short blurb about your speaking topic as it relates to your book. Organize an outline of bulleted points to be covered in your talk. Make sure you have interesting or insightful things to say that will interest an audience. Then prepare to market your speaking availability to the local community. Update your research and cite sources appropriately. Prepare a brochure or short mailer that describes your topics and your background. You can purchase email lists or regular mailing lists through which your brochures can be distributed. For more information about how to prepare a speaker's promotional kit, visit our website at www.writeitGodsway.com.

Start with a smaller group of people where you are known or have something in common, like your church or a community civic group. Volunteer to give a short talk on your topic while linking it to the group for which you will be speaking. For example, if you are writing a book on helping teens to choose a ministry, you can give a talk to the teens' Sunday school class or to their parents' class to offer helpful tips. Then market your presentation to the Rotary, Lions' Club, or another local group that is interested in the topic. Keep your talk brief, focused, and informative. Sprinkle in light humor, but offer useful facts and suggestions. Prepare a handout that includes mention of your book:

Sample presentation title:

"Equipping Teens for Ministry" by John Doe, author of *Raising Compassionate Teens* (add publishing date).

The more you are willing to make free public appearances, the more likely you are to get your name known as an expert on your topic. Newspaper editors may contact you for an interview if you don't contact them first to offer one. Free publicity of this kind attracts potential buyers for the book when it becomes available, as readers like to buy books from authors they know, especially from those who give public service presentations and free useful advice.

Two helpful organizations where you can learn to become a polished speaker and practice your presentation skills are with the Toastmasters International (www.Toastmasters.org) and the National Speakers

Association (www.NSAspeaker.org). Visiting these websites or joining these speakers' organizations will bring you in contact with other speakers and provide you with a wealth of information and experience.

While building your credentials as an author/speaker and infopreneur, you will learn more about the topic from your audiences, based on questions they ask or suggestions they make. If you cannot answer a question, you have the opportunity to research the topic further and include that information in your book as you write it, knowing that some readers will expect to find those facts or opinion therein. You also will get a feel for the topics that the audience finds most relevant or interesting; then you can capitalize on these as you finish the book and maybe play down the parts that readers find less interesting or relevant. This "test marketing" approach can be very useful as your book approaches publication.

The Bible, published in parts, became a reference point for believers in the Old Testament and New Testament. The faithful searched the Word diligently for answers to everyday problems and spiritual dilemmas:

> *"Now these [Jews] were better disposed and more noble than those in Thessalonica, for they were entirely ready and accepted and welcomed the message [concerning the attainment through Christ of eternal salvation in the kingdom of God] with inclination of mind and eagerness, searching and examining the Scriptures daily to see if these things were so."*
> *—Acts 17:11 AMP*

As you develop expertise in your topic, and perhaps go on to write more books on related topics, you will establish a market niche that readers will come to anticipate and appreciate. As an author, you will become familiar with your strengths and weaknesses, preferences and dislikes, in choosing and refining topics for speaking and publishing. Readers will associate you with writing certain kinds of books, and they will come to you first for information about related topics. A publisher might even approach you to ask if you would consider writing about a particular subject of interest.

As you develop confidence in your topic and your knowledge, you will have more clarity about whether to publish your book with a commercial publishing house, allowing the experts to make most of the marketing decisions, or whether you feel comfortable in taking risks to publish your own book. Much will depend on the contacts you make and the connections you have in getting the word out about your new book. While you will have to trust God for the ultimate outcome, be sure to do all you can to ensure the success of your writing and publishing ministry by becoming informed and making wise choices.

Honor the Lord with Your First Fruits

While it may seem premature to start planning your tithing strategy based on profits from your still-to-be-published book, this is actually a very good time to consider God's direction for your publishing ministry, and to prepare to honor Him by tithing from your book income. Naturally, the amount given to God remains a confidential agreement between Him and each author. But it is important to keep in mind that is through God and by His will that we are able to write and have work published for His glory and our benefit.

See what the Bible teaches about giving to our God:

> *"Will a man rob or defraud God? Yet you rob and defraud Me. But you say, 'In what way do we rob or defraud You?' '[You have withheld your] tithes and offerings.*
>
> *'You are cursed with the curse, for you are robbing Me, even this whole nation. (Lev. 26:14-17.] Bring all the tithes (the whole tenth of your income) into the storehouse, that there may be food in My house, and prove Me now by it, says the Lord of hosts, if I will not open the windows of heaven for you and pour you out a blessing, that there shall not be room enough to receive it. [Mal. 2:2]*
>
> *'And I will rebuke the devourer [insects and plagues] for your sakes and he shall not destroy the fruits of your ground, neither shall your vine drop its fruit before the time in the field,' says the Lord of hosts.*
>
> *And all nations shall call you happy and blessed, for you shall be a land of delight,' says the Lord of hosts."*
> *—Malachi 3:8-12 AMP*

It is not only the work of our hands that pleases the Lord, but also the gain, or payment that we receive from our labor, when we respectfully commit a portion of our earnings to the Lord through tithes and offerings. How can God bless a writing ministry when an author fails to respect Biblical teachings in the important area of finance? Moreover, why should He choose to bless a writing ministry that does not keep Him first in the plan and the payoff from the writing? He knows the best uses for our tithes, so why not let God make the decision of how to spend that portion of our earnings?

No one should have to struggle and scrape together the money owed God. Rather, God's portion should come off the top of our earnings as a priority; whether from gross or net income is up to the individual.

> *"The first of the first fruits of your ground you shall bring into the house of the Lord your God."*
> *—Exodus 23:19(A) AMP*

As your writing becomes successful and sought after, you might even decide to donate occasional pieces to Christian publications to offer your talent to the Lord by giving to smaller Christian magazines that cannot afford to offer payment. Donating a published piece of writing to help a ministry's website or magazine is a generous use of your writing gift. Honoring God first and enriching ourselves second is a good habit to cultivate as you develop this talent for evangelistic purposes.

> *"Give, and [gifts] will be given to you: good measure, pressed down, shaken together, and running over, will they pour into [the pouch formed by] the bosom [of your robe and used as a bag]. For with the measure you deal out [with the measure you use when you confer benefits on others], it will be measured back to you."*
> *—Luke 6:38 AMP*

You may have heard the saying, "You can't out-give God." Many Christians bear testimony to this truth when they give the best portion of their income and then watch in amazement as God blesses them many times over. There is no guarantee that you will receive more material gain than you donate, because God's blessings come in many sizes and shapes, and most are far more valuable than mere dollars and cents. But when we put our talent and its monetary reward into His capable Hands, we know they will be used in the best possible way and that God will bless us somehow, some way, for trusting Him in this important way.

Summary

Commercial publishing offers the advantage of having professionals do most of the work for you in preparing, printing, and promoting your book to the public. On the other hand, self-publishing lets you control the publishing process. Weigh the pros and cons of each method as you start thinking about which method will best serve your ministry in getting the message to readers. You may want to call both types of publishing companies or visit their websites for more information about each type of publishing program so that you can make a truly informed decision about publishing your writing.

Writer's Wisdom:

What is the best way to launch my book into the world for effective ministry?

For Revelation:

"So they went out and preached that men should repent [that they should change their minds for the better and heartily amend their ways, with abhorrence of their past sins]."
—Mark 6:12 AMP

The Master's Writing Plan Activities
Writing Step #1:

Write a paragraph describing reasons for self-publishing versus commercial publishing. Review your list to help decide which route to take.
Writing Step #2:

Make a tentative list of ministries and organizations where you might be able to give a short talk on some aspect of your book's topic. Eventually you will need to add the name of a contact person and begin calling to volunteer as a speaker at a class or church event.
Writing Step #3:

Visit websites of self-publishing companies that print on demand (POD) to compare publishing packages for your book. Take into account auxiliary services like editing help, cover design, and marketing options. Create a list of the top three to keep in mind for the future.

New Testament Reading Plan Week #4:

Luke 1 to Luke 13

Chapter Five

Build on a Rock

Develop Your Book's Ideas

*"He is like a man building a house, who dug and went down deep and
laid a foundation upon the rock; and when a flood arose, the torrent
broke against that house and could not shake or move it, because it had
been securely built or founded on a rock."*
—Luke 6:48 AMP

Maybe you feel as though writing a book should be creatively inspired, not logically planned. You wait for that tiny spark of talent to blaze into a bonfire of productivity. Day by day, your disappointment grows as you become concerned that your book will never get written. It's a great idea, but...

Forget the "but" and get to work. How? Just do it. Sit down and write your book, one word at a time, forming sentences, paragraphs, and whole pages of information that will help your readers to improve their lives by applying your insightful principles and practices. After all, that's why you decided to pen a book, right? You feel strongly that you have something to share with readers everywhere. So get busy and get started.

As suggested by the opening parable in Luke 6:48 AMP, all Godly work should be built on the rock of faith. Imagine what would have happened if people like Noah, Abraham, Moses, and Daniel had followed God's commands half-heartedly, waiting for some kind of anticipated spiritual inspiration to motivate them to complete obedience. Obviously,

God's divine inspiration would and did arrive, but perhaps not in the form or timeline these Godly men had anticipated.

Poor Noah built a ship in the middle of a dry region without even a drop of rain to inspire him. And the boat was huge—not some little canoe to be worked on behind his town home. No, the ark was so big that people in the community must have noticed it and undoubtedly scoffed at the consistent efforts of their unusual neighbor. Noah's commitment paid off in a big way when only he, his wife and sons and his son's wives were saved from the flood that destroyed the entire earth, although it must have seemed at times as though he were on a fool's errand. It is possible he doubted himself and questioned God's ability to carry out His decree. But faith literally saved the lives of Noah and his trusting family.

Aging Abraham was told at the age of 100 to expect a child to be born of his 90-year-old wife, Sarah, despite the fact that at Sarah's urging, Abraham had conceived a son by her Egyptian handmaid, Hagar:

> *"Then Abraham fell on his face and laughed and said in his heart, 'Shall a child be born to a man who is a hundred years old? And shall Sarah, who is ninety years old, bear a son?'"*
> *—Genesis 17:17 AMP*

The announcement of Isaac's birth certainly required a leap of faith to two elderly people well past their childbearing years. But God knew His man well—Abraham was right for the job and Sarah's body was rejuvenated! The Godly pair accepted the pronouncement and proudly welcomed son Isaac into the world.

Moses, a stuttering shepherd who had made Pharaoh's most wanted list for murder, stood up to the King of Egypt not once, but several times, to foretell God's curses on the disobedient kingdom. Obviously, his leadership demanded great courage and fortitude at the risk of self-sacrifice. Bolstered by God's guidance and Aaron's support, Moses followed through and led the Children of Israel to the Promised Land of Israel.

The prophet Daniel was thrown into a fiery furnace and fed to wild lions—yet escaped these perils to experience God's amazing revelation that Daniel wrote to enlighten others concerning future events. His extraordinary vision left Daniel in mourning for three weeks:

"In the third year of Cyrus king of Persia a word was revealed to Daniel, who was called Belteshazzar. And the word was true and it referred to great tribulation (conflict and wretchedness). And he understood the word and had understanding of the vision [Dan. 8:26; Rev. 19:9.]

In those days I, Daniel, was mourning for three whole weeks.

I ate no pleasant or desirable food, nor did any meat or wine come into my mouth and I did not anoint myself at all for the full three weeks."

—Daniel 10:1-3 AMP

"And behold, one in the likeness of the sons of men touched my lips. Then I opened my mouth and spoke. I said to him who stood before me, 'O my lord, by reason of the vision sorrows and pains have come upon me, and I retain no strength.

"For how can my lord's servant [who is so feeble] talk with this my lord? For now no strength remains in me, nor is there any breath left in me."

—Daniel 10:16, 17 AMP

God's truth does not come easily. It demands a heavy price. If your book is guided by Biblical principles, you may labor to communicate its truths. Each of the leaders mentioned above paid a price for their spiritual leadership and insight. But as you strive to record your ideas in tangible form, you will experience the satisfaction and peace that comes from meaningful self-expression in writing your book God's way.

Writing is challenging work. It requires consistent effort and enormous patience. You need to write on a schedule, just as you would handle any other type of job or project. Give yourself an area in which to work, preferably with few interruptions or distractions. The following tips offer practical advice for bringing your ideas to life in the form of a rough draft, which will be the starting point of your book.

1. Arrange personal writing space.

If you don't have an existing home office or work area, set one up now. You can probably get by with a desk, a computer or paper and pen, good lighting, and privacy. God talked to His chosen leaders in personal or even secretive locations: Abraham and Moses in the wilderness, Noah and

Daniel away from their neighbors' prying eyes, and other Old Testament prophets in isolated areas where others could not see or interrupt. Jesus spent 40 days alone in the wilderness preparing for His ministry. Find a quiet place away from the family where you can work in solitude and listen for God's still, small voice.

2. Work from your brainstorming activities or outline.

God equipped His servants with a message that they would then craft to suit their particular audiences. The same holds true for Christian writers. Start with a preliminary sketch of your book's idea, and then develop a rough draft that will begin to shape up into individual chapters. Feel free to change your original plan as needed; flexibility is essential to tailor your message to meet readers' expectations.

3. Let the ideas flow.

God's plans always begin with action. A spiritual being speaks; a human responds and usually does something to help others. People interact, often in conflict, as God's message is relayed to its intended audience. The Bible doesn't tell many stories of prophets sitting around thinking about how to deliver a message or make a point. They just did it in a straightforward manner. Follow their example with your book's idea. Just let the writing flow in an unstructured way to get lots of words on the screen or page before you. Later, you will have plenty of time to rearrange your phrasing and make corrections.

4. Write creatively to generate ideas and information.

The world we live in today does not seem much to resemble the original earth as described in Genesis 1. Although God created and assembled all the pieces that would be used, He later rearranged those pieces, removing some (like the Garden of Eden) and adding others (such as barren deserts) to adjust the landscape in new patterns. Similarly, as you begin writing your draft, create as much information as you need for each section, but don't slow down to give much thought to what you are writing just yet. Simply write about the idea of a particular section or chapter as completely as possible. For example, if your book discusses how to be supportive of single parents in a church, list everything you can think of, from childcare to car repairs, home-cooked meals, and educational support. Later, when you go back through the draft and begin revising, you can decide which ideas to leave in, and which ones to take out. At that point, you might have more ideas to add. The first draft, called 'creative writing,' is based on transferring information in the form of ideas from your head to the page before you.

5. Critically evaluate your preliminary information.
Most authors who examine their writing with a critical, or watchful, eye will find many opportunities for improving it, unlike God, whose original creation of the Earth was perfect and didn't need to be edited:

> *"And God saw everything that He had made, and behold, it was very good (suitable, pleasant) and He approved it completely..."*
> *—Genesis 1:31(A) AMP*

We human writers must take time to honestly assess what we've written and look for ways to make it better. After completing a rough draft of one of your book's sections, let it sit a day or so. Then read the draft with "fresh eyes" for a clearer impression. Now you are ready to add, remove, or change some of the ideas with which you began in preparation for rewriting the next draft of that section.

Check your rough draft for the following:

1 Does your book glorify God?
2 Does the draft develop the chapter's main point or idea?
3 If the main point changes in the draft, does it still link to the rest of the book?
4 Are the main points supported by examples, description, or other evidence?
5 Does the chapter have an introduction, developed ideas, and a conclusion?
6 Is each paragraph based on its own topic idea? Do they link to each other?
7 Have you correctly cited research and well-known facts?
8 Are your tone, diction, and vocabulary appropriate for the topic?
9 Does your grammar appear to be mostly accurate?

In the New Testament, the analogy of a vine defines those who are "born" in the family of God's chosen people (Jews) and those who are grafted in (Christians). All believers are connected through faith in Christ.

> *"I am the Vine; you are the branches. Whoever lives in Me and I in him bears much (abundant) fruit. However, apart from Me [cut off from vital union with Me] you can do nothing."*
> —*John 15:5 AMP*

Similarly, the ideas in each chapter of your book should be distinct and clearly defined, but they also need to be connected to the other chapters, and overall, to the book's main point, for individual chapters to be effective. After developing several chapters, if one appears not to fit in with the others, you will have to "prune" it through revision or deletion.

Getting started is the most difficult step of writing a book, for many authors. That's why it is so important to force yourself to get started and to stay motivated. Even if you write just three pages daily, in three months you will have nearly 300 pages. Each word on the page is like a drop in the bucket; soon, your pail will be overflowing with more than enough information to share with enthralled readers.

Don't worry about your first draft being perfect or complete. After writing it, letting it sit, reviewing for general accuracy and development, and making basic corrections, you are ready to move on to the next chapter. One by one, stay on track as you develop each chapter's substance by exploring its core idea. Together, each chapter will link to others to form a strand of interlocking topics that develop your book's principal idea.

When you have a rough draft for each chapter, along with the general development of the overall concept for your book, you will be ready to move on to the next phase of your project.

Writer's Wisdom:
What is the best way to develop my book's idea into a first draft?

For Revelation:
"But he who practices truth [who does what is right] comes out into the Light; so that his works may be plainly shown to be what

they are—wrought with God [divinely prompted, done with God's help, in dependence upon Him]."
—John 3:21 AMP

The Master's Writing Plan Activities
Writing Step #1:
Write a rough draft of your first chapter, using your outline, notes, and research that were collected for Chapter Three writing activities. Don't think about accuracy or smoothness right now. Just get your ideas on paper where you can polish them later.

Writing Step #2:
After completing the chapter's rough draft, let it sit a day or two, giving yourself time away from the writing so that you can re-read it objectively later.

Writing Step #3:
Now return to your rough draft and read it carefully. Look for vagueness, errors, and other problems that need to be changed or fixed. Make general corrections to support the chapter's main idea.

New Testament Reading Plan Week #5:
Luke 14 to John 10

Chapter Six

Don't Think About the Weeds

"And the servants of the owner came to him and said, Sir, did you not sow good seed in your field? Then how does it have darnel shoots in it? He replied to them, An enemy has done this. The servants said to him, Then do you want us to go and weed them out? But he said, No, lest in gathering the wild wheat (weeds resembling wheat), you root up the [true] wheat along with it. Let them grow together until the harvest; and at harvest time I will say to the reapers, Gather the darnel first and bind it in bundles to be burned, but gather the wheat into my granary."
—Matthew 13:27-30 AMP

So far in the first half of this book, we've discussed how to focus your message and begin writing by developing each main idea into its own chapter. As you describe your feelings, experiences, research, and insight in each section, you may find misspellings, incorrect punctuation or grammar, or incomplete information. These discoveries can make you want to stop writing and go back to start editing. But it is more important at first to get your ideas in print than to make sure every word is absolutely correct. Accuracy is important, and we will get to that eventually. For now, just put your ideas into words on the computer screen or in print so they begin to make sense. As in the parable of the weeds discussed in Matthew 13 above, there is a season when you can afford to overlook the "weeds" in your writing, knowing full well that you will return at some point to uproot them.

There are many stories in Scripture that remind us to bypass errors temporarily while maintaining momentum with the main strategy—in this case, writing your story. For example, King David tolerated the curses of Shimei, son of Gera, while re-establishing his kingdom, before instructing successor Solomon to take revenge. Later, God tolerated the Israelites' infidelities of prolific idol worship until the eventual Babylonian captivity. This is not to say that we should permanently refuse to deal with any weaknesses or problems in our writing. Rather, we should make it a priority to complete each chapter before thinking about the final details.

The writing process, when followed, provides opportunities to create, develop, and fine-tune your ideas.

1 **Prewriting**—also called **invention**—is the beginning stage of a writing project when you begin to write simply to get words on paper, or a computer screen. This can take the form of an outline, list, or cluster of information that will become the basis of your book.

2 **Drafting**—producing a rough draft—is the second stage of the writing process. This is when an author takes the original notes, lists, or other ideas and starts knitting them together to create a useful tapestry of information.

3 **Revising**—viewed mainly as editing—is the final stage of writing when an author returns to the work after a brief lapse to review the material with a "cool" eye, or detached mindset that will reveal flaws, weaknesses, and mistakes. Using a grammar guide or style sheet, the writer will be able to check rules and locate problems that can be corrected in the final run-through.

"He who has knowledge spares his words, and a man of under-standing has a cool spirit. [James 1:19."]
—Proverbs 17:27 AMP

Just as God provides second chances, be kind to yourself in planning to write several drafts before the book is finally ready for a publisher. Don't expect your book to come together smoothly and seamlessly in a single writing. Most likely, you will have to spend time combing through it, once written, to check and double-check areas that seem questionable, weak, or undeveloped.

> *"[We pray] that you may be invigorated and strengthened with*
> *all power according to the might of His glory, [to exercise] every*
> *kind of endurance and patience (perseverance and forbearance)*
> *with joy"*
> —*Colossians 1:11 AMP*

Structuring a First Draft

Earlier chapters of this book guided you through choosing a topic, designating main points as chapter topics, and beginning to write. As you put your thoughts into expression that other people will read, it is important to create a sense of organization, with each topic (chapter) linking to the next in a recognizable order. Although you don't have to be concerned about including all the details and examples you eventually plan to use, you will want to establish a framework for your book that allows your ideas to unfold in a clear manner.

Many books develop sections like the following:

1   The introduction includes an overview of the message and the main points that will be explored in each chapter.

2   A related section of the Introduction or the chapter that follows often provides a history or background of your topic, explaining approximately when, where, and how it became an issue. Also to be found in this section are diverse viewpoints offering conflicting perspectives or alternate points of view to show the author's well-rounded familiarity with the topic overall.

3   Examples are revealed in each chapter. These either provide evidence for the book's message, or they display various aspects of the main idea.

4   A conclusion summarizes the message, restates the main ideas, and/or offers a principle of application for readers.

As you work through your information, organize it, and set it down in print as your first draft, you will automatically add Scripture verses, explanations, details, and descriptions that come to mind as you are thinking about that part of the book. If you are working from a well-developed set of handwritten or typed notes, you may have fewer spontaneous thoughts to add, but chances are that additional points will come to mind, so feel free to include this information as well. The important thing is to keep at it until your project is finished, keeping God's purposes in mind:

> *"Let your character or moral disposition be free from love of money[including greed, avarice, lust, and craving for earthly possessions] and be satisfied with your present [circumstances and what you have]; for He [God] Himself has said, 'I will not in any way fail you nor give you up nor leave you without support. [I will] not, [I will] not, [I will] not in any degree leave you helpless nor forsake nor let [you] down (relax My hold on you) [Assuredly not!] [Josh. 1:5.]"*
> *—Hebrews 13:5 AMP*

A rough draft will not be perfectly written from start to finish. It is merely a way to begin writing your book that provides a plan for developing the ideas through several subsequent drafts. Just as a baker mixes up piecrust dough by adding a series of ingredients, sometimes modifying those items slightly to get the right texture, so will your rough draft begin to emerge from an assortment of ideas and approaches. Most bakers mix up extra piecrust dough so they have a little more than is needed to work with. This makes it easier to roll out the dough and spread it over the pie pan for even coverage before the overhanging edges are trimmed away. The same can hold true for writers. It is a good idea to plan on assembling plenty of information, even if you are not sure all of it will be needed, so you can eliminate the excess once you find you have enough.

Even early Church evangelicals didn't have their message 100% ready and fixed as they began their ministries. Peter, for example, soon was challenged for his teachings that new believers must first adopt Jewish customs like circumcision before becoming Christians. The Old Testament law of keeping kosher became obsolete after Peter experienced a vision that commanded him to consider all foods clean for Jews, possibly in keeping with his role of evangelist in ministering to Gentles and traditionally "unclean" peoples, since sharing meals would become a strategic way of sharing their faith. The important goal is to persevere in completing your book as a sacrificial offering to God and a ministry offering to fellow believers:

> *"The next day as they were still on their way and were approaching the town, Peter went up to the roof of the house to pray, about the sixth hour(noon).*
>
> *But be became very hungry, and wanted something to eat; and while the meal was being prepared a trance came over him.*
>
> *And he saw the sky opened and something like a great sheet lowered by the four corners, descending to the earth.*
>
> *It contained all kinds of quadrupeds and wild beasts and creeping things of the earth and birds of the air.*
>
> *And there came a voice to him, saying, Rise up, Peter, kill and eat.*
>
> *But Peter said, No, by no means, Lord: for I have never eaten anything that is common and unhallowed or [ceremonially] unclean.*
>
> *And the voice came to him again a second time, What God has cleansed and pronounced clean, do not you defile and profane by regarding and calling common and unhallowed or unclean.*
>
> *This occurred three times; then immediately the sheet was taken up to heaven.*
>
> *And Peter opened his mouth and said: Most certainly and thoroughly I now perceive and understand that God shows no partiality and is no respecter of persons."*
> *—Acts 10:9-16, 34 AMP*

> *"That is why I would remind you to stir up (rekindle the embers of, fan the flame of, and keep burning) the [gracious] gift of God, [the inner fire] that is in you by means of the laying on of my hands [with those of the elders at your ordination].*
>
> *"For God did not give us a spirit of timidity (of cowardice, of craven and cringing and fawning fear), but [He has given us a spirit] of power and of love and of calm and well-balanced mind and discipline and self-control.*
>
> *"Do not blush or be ashamed then, to testify to and for our Lord, nor of me, a prisoner for His sake, but [with me] take your*

*share of the suffering [to which the preaching] of the Gospel [may
expose you, and do it] in the power of God."*
—2 Timothy 1:6-8 AMP

Human evangelical messages, whether presented orally or in print,
generally have room for improvement at almost every level. Certainly, a
new writer who is in the initial stage of recording ideas to be published in a
book, will want to create a first draft, set it aside, and return to it later after
a few days of respite to reconsider what has been written, and to look for
ways to improve or enhance the message in a second draft.

Don't Whack Those Weeds Yet
As you work to capture the essence of your message in words that
will bind them to the page, don't be concerned at first about relatively
minor details like spelling, capitalization, punctuation, grammar, and word
choices. These are called "syntax," and they can be dealt with later, after
you have gotten your ideas in print. At that point you can use reference tools
like a dictionary and thesaurus to check for accuracy and smoothness.

After you have written the draft, set it aside for a day or two at least.
Then you can return to the draft with a "fresh eye" to review what you have
written and see how it sounds now. You may feel that the draft sounds
terrific, and even take pleasure in finding that your ideas come across as
clearly as you hoped. Or you might find opportunities for improvement—
adding a half sentence here, changing a word or phrase there, or even
writing in another paragraph or two to clearify the concept in question.

Don't sweat the small stuff. It's too soon to think about proofreading
and surface errors. These can be addressed in the revising stage after you
complete the entire book.

Instead, during the drafting stage of the writing process, focus on
"semantics," which refers to your message and the ideas you want to share
with readers to help them understand a vital concept or even to take action
that can change lives. These are your primary goals for writing the first
draft of each chapter, so it is important to emphasize substance over style
in the first draft of each chapter.

Sometimes a writer will struggle with self-expression. "How should I
say this?" "How much do I say?" "How can I make people understand my
point of view?" These are all legitimate questions for a writer, and they can

be considered while planning the book or as it begins to take form during the rough draft stage. You can keep a log of questions or suggestions to return to later after you have completed a first full draft of your manuscript. Segment these by chapter number so you can readily find areas that need attention when you come back for revision and correction.

Just keep on writing to say what you need to in each chapter. Don't think about the final draft yet. That stage will come soon enough. If you run out of steam, stop writing temporarily and do something else. Later, when your mind calms down and refocuses on your book, return with a calm spirit and begin writing again. Motivate yourself to write a few words about the topic you are working on. Don't give up! Just as Jesus sent His disciples out, two by two, to share His redemptive message without preparation or extra supplies, you can take the same approach to writing, especially when you get stuck. Just do it—and the ideas will follow your fingers.

Writer's Wisdom:
What is the best way for God to inspire my writing of this book?

For Revelation:
"He charged them to take nothing for their journey except a walking stick—no bread, no wallet for a collection bag, no money in their belts (girdles, purses)"
—Mark 6:8 AMP

The Master's Writing Plan Activities
Writing Step #1:
Review what you have written so far. Mainly explore the ideas and your sense of direction. Is each chapter relatively solid, based on a central point that is supported by Biblical revelation? If you have concerns, rewrite that section until it agrees with the Word.

Writing Step #2:
After looking over your completed writing as instructed in the previous chapter, print out a draft of each chapter and use a color ink pen (so it will show up readily) to mark areas that need to be checked or corrected for

biblical principles, clarity, or support. Don't think about proofreading yet, just focus on your main ideas and how they will come across to readers.

Writing Step #3:

Now read the marked-up chapters closely, following your two sets of rewrites from the last chapter and this one. Again, at this point don't be concerned about "pulling weeds" that spring from technical grammar rules; you can address these later. Just make sure the main idea of each chapter is solid and Biblically supported. Then you will be ready to move on.

New Testament Reading Plan Week #6:

John 11 through Acts 8

Chapter Seven

Fulfill the Promise

"[He has also appropriated and acknowledged us as His by] putting His seal upon us and giving us His [Holy] Spirit in our hearts as the security deposit and guarantee [of the fulfillment of His promise]."
—*2 Corinthians 1:22 AMP*

As a believer, you undoubtedly have made God the center of your life and sought His guidance in writing your book. The Bible is very important to you, so why shouldn't it be important for your readers as well? How can anything you write not have the Bible's truths at its core?

Whatever type of book you are authoring, it is important to find ways to instill biblical truths in your message in subtle but significant ways. You don't want to hit your readers over the head, but you don't want them to miss the point, either. Striking a balance between structure and suggestiveness is delicate. This chapter will help to explain how to do it without compromising your integrity as a Christian or as an author:

"For our appeal [in preaching] does not [originate] from delusion, or error or impure purpose or motive, nor in fraud or deceit.

But just as we have been approved by God to be entrusted with the glad tidings (the Gospel), so we speak not to please men but to please God, Who tests our hearts [expecting them to be approved].

For as you well know, we never resorted either to words of flattery or to any cloak to conceal greedy motives or pretexts for gain, [as] God is our witness.

Nor did we seek to extract praise and honor and glory from men, either from you or from anyone else, though we might have asserted our authority [stood on our dignity and claimed honor] as apostles (special missionaries) of Christ (the Messiah)."
—*I Thessalonians 2:3-6 AMP*

What is Your Point?

In the first half of this book, we have been talking about the importance of honing your message until it is clear and sharp. You want readers to understand the main idea, but you hope they will appreciate it on their own, through the natural flow of information in your book. Some truths must be thrashed out; others are delicately explained. When you feel your message will make Biblical sense to most readers, you are ready to move on to the next chapter. But an important part of making each chapter speak to your audience is the spiritual kernel buried within.

There's not much point to sharing useful information with readers if they will only use it to get ahead in this world. That's not our goal as Christians. Rather, we want to make them aware of the transitory nature of this world, and guide them into a quest for meaning in the next world, the spiritual domain. Your thoughtfully crafted chapters should Biblically and gracefully build on one another to create meaning that will lead your audience to the truths that you have prepared for them. By the end of each chapter, readers should be pondering a principle that you have introduced as a result of the chapter's discussion.

For example, a book about witnessing in the workplace could address potential obstacles in each chapter: management, hostile coworkers, a secular environment, your place in the company's hierarchy, and so on. Each chapter would develop a discussion of an obstacle and then present ways of overcoming it, perhaps drawing on real-life examples, research, or personal experience. Not only will readers have helpful general principles to work from by the end of each chapter, but they also will be ready to learn more about managing workplace barriers to evangelism in the next chapter. Each chapter leads into or links with the succeeding one. In this type of book, the spiritual principles are Jesus' command to preach the

Gospel throughout the world, so the biblical truth is clear-cut and straight-forward. Remember, our mission is the Great Commission!

> *"Jesus approached and, breaking the silence, said to them, Al authority (all power of rule) in heaven and on earth has been given to Me.*
> *Go then and make disciples of all the nations, baptizing them into the name of the Father and of the Son and of the Holy Spirit.*
> *Teaching them to observe everything that I have commanded you, and behold, I am with you all the days (perpetually, uniformly, and on every occasion), to the [very] close and consummation of the age, Amen (so let it be)."*
> *—Matthew 28:18-20*

But in another type of book, one that is not necessarily published by a Christian publisher but is intended to impact readers from all walks of life with spiritual truths, you would take a different approach. Let's say you want to write a book about the value of honesty in the workplace. Everyone should be honest, not just Christians, so this book is for everyone who is interested in workplace honesty. You could address many interesting facets of job-site honesty and dishonesty, including statistics on white-collar crime, the history and examples of dishonesty among employees and its cost to the company, as well as how employees can establish integrity and build meaningful careers by embracing workplace ethics. Instead of using Bible scriptures in each chapter, you could embed a spiritual truth without citing Scripture, except occasionally, perhaps, as in reciting the Golden Rule or a biblical parable or story. Many business authors today use their faith as a springboard for workplace ethics and get results that have impacted companies around the globe when readers respond in positive ways.

Christian authors cannot hide their light under a bushel. The flicker from their message based on biblical values will shine forth from the pages of their books to illuminate the lives of readers for reflection and application:

> *"For God did not give us a spirit of timidity (of cowardice, of craven and cringing and fawning fear), but [He has given us a*

*spirit] of power and of love and of calm and well-balanced mind
and discipline and self-control."*
—*II Timothy 1:7 AMP*

Light Your Readers' World

Whatever your goals in writing a book, you will want to consider ways
in which you can enlighten readers about Christianity. There are many
strategies you can use to bring spiritual matters to the attention of your
readers. Here are some common methods:

1. Under chapter headings, add well-known Bible sayings or
   verses, like the Golden Rule, one of the Ten Commandments,
   or a Proverb. Many people have heard of these and will not feel
   "preached at" because the sayings are common knowledge and
   often found throughout Western society. God's Word does not go
   void. Sharing Scriptures in your writing can leave an imprint on
   people's souls, even if you are sharing small snippets.
2. Summarize a biblical truth without citing specific verses. Everyone
   knows the story of the Prodigal Son as told by Jesus, and using the
   term "prodigal" should click instantly with most readers. If you
   manage to excite their interest with your reference, some may be
   encouraged to look up more information online or in the Bible,
   and thus begin to search out Biblical truth for themselves.
3. Cite global leaders or celebrities who are Christians or who rely
   on Christian principles for success. Zig Ziglar, John C. Maxwell,
   and Bob Harrison are among dozens of household success names
   that have been known to espouse biblical views. Including their
   names and their views provides additional links to the Bible for
   your readers.
4. Avoid including references to more than one world faith, trusting
   God to make Christianity stand apart as His chosen pillar of faith.
   People who normally get turned off by reading about the Bible
   may be more open-minded to your positive view of Christianity,
   especially if you complicate your message by discussing other
   faiths.
5. Paraphrase biblical passages that may subconsciously echo in
   Bible verses readers have heard previously, especially as children.

Without using quotation marks or citations, you can incorporate Scripture to sound very natural and yet allow the Holy Spirit to work through the biblical passages to touch the hearts of your reading audience.

When offering Christ to a secular world, a writer will need to use wisdom to get past anti-Christian gatekeepers who try to repel and discredit Christianity in a godless society. Christian books can march through the gates of publication openly; secular books must look for a back door. Either type of book can have a tremendous impact when it is well written and rooted in biblical truths.

What Motivates You?

Take a few minutes to think about the books you have read that left an impact on you since the time you were a child. Christian or secular, what makes these books special? Why do they stand out in your memory? What spiritual truths or biblical lessons did you learn from them?

Now consider how your book compares to those that impress you. Have you borrowed from these influences? Are you using similar techniques? It is not wrong to write your book in a parallel style as long as you don't copy, or plagiarize, others' ideas and information. Are you able to shut out worldly influences?

"O Timothy, guard and keep the deposit entrusted [to you]! Turn away from the irreverent babble and godless chatter, with the vain and empty and worldly phrases, and the subtleties and the contradictions in what is falsely called knowledge and spiritual illumination."
—I Timothy 6:20 AMP

Of all the millions of books in the world today, only a few are destined for greatness. Some of these will become enormously popular because of a celebrity's endorsement. Others will become the beneficiaries of an outstanding market campaign that capitalizes on current social interests and consumer needs. Still other books, a very small percentage of the best sellers, will touch the hearts of readers around the globe to strike a responsive chord. Well written and well researched, these few classics will last for ages to come as representations of our civilization's most profound minds and deepest sentiments.

While your publishing goals may not include becoming a top seller or reaching millions of readers, these outcomes are not bad in themselves, as they would help to move your message around the globe to people everywhere who need to hear it. But most books serve a more specific readership and accomplish localized goals.

> *"All things have been entrusted and delivered to Me by My Father; and no one fully knows and accurately understands the Son except the Father and no one fully knows and accurately understands the Father except the Son and anyone to whom the Son deliberately wills to make Him known.*
>
> *Come to Me, all you who labor and are heavy-laden and over-burdened, and I will cause you to rest. [I will ease and relieve and refresh your souls.]*
> *—Matthew 11:27-28 AMP*

To get your book published and in the hands of those who need to hear its message, you will have to craft your ideas to attract reader attention and touch either their heart or their head—and maybe both. Even if your message reaches a single reader whose faith is enriched as a result, you have done the job entrusted to you in publishing your book. As we all know, it only takes one domino to create a far-reaching effect. One author who publishes a notable message may touch the life of one reader whose actions will impact the lives of thousands.

> *"What do you think? If a man has a hundred sheep, and one of them has gone astray and gets lost, will he not leave the ninety-nine on the mountain and go in search of the one that is lost?*
>
> *And if it should be that he finds it, truly I say to you, he rejoices more over it than over the ninety-nine that did not get lost.*
>
> *Just so it is not the will of My Father Who is in heaven that one of these little ones should be lost and perish."*
> *—Matthew 18:12-14 AMP*

Choose Scriptural support with prayer. Weave it through your words with wisdom. Pray for God's leading, and watch miracles begin to happen. Christian authors have an obligation to present God's truth as clearly as possible. Yet, the world at large will try to ignore, avoid, or dismantle the truth, which can make it difficult to get close-minded people to read it. Reflect on the steps you can take to share your message with people who don't want to hear it, along with those who do. Trust God for the outcomes:

> *"And we are now writing these things to you so that our joy [in seeing you included] may be full [and your joy may be complete]."*
> —*I John 1:4 AMP*

Writer's Wisdom:
What are the spiritual truths I want to share in my book?

For Revelation:
> *"The fruit of the [uncompromisingly] righteous is a tree of life, and he who is wise captures human lives [for God, as a fisher of men—he gathers and receives them for eternity]. [Matt.4:19; I Cor. 9:19, James 5:20.]*
> —*Proverbs 11:30 AMP*

The Master's Writing Plan Activities
Writing Step #1:
Go back through each chapter draft you have written so far. Underline or highlight the Christian views that are outlined either subtly or specifically. Then look for biblical references, overt or covert, and do the same. Compare these to the end of your chapter to see if they build up to a spiritual insight that your readers will grasp. If not, revise the areas that lead to these truths so your readers will readily recognize them.

Writing Step #2:
In reviewing your proposed chapter titles, some of which are already developed, and others which have yet to be written, make a list of the Scriptures or principles that you plan to incorporate, or those you already

have. Read through the written chapters to see if these references, oblique or not, offer grains of Biblical truth that readers will appreciate. If you cannot easily locate them, or if you are unsure whether readers will be able to readily find them, revise those sections to make them sharper and clearer. Consider stylistic effects like bullet points, numbering, italics, or bolded fonts so that the Scriptures will catch your readers' eye.

Writing Step #3:

Write down a summary verse that you want to represent the final truth for your book. Check the other Scriptures you are using in each chapter to make sure they lead up to and link with your summary Scripture.

New Testament Reading Plan Week #7:

Acts 9 through Acts 26

Chapter Eight

Make Your Paths Straight

"And cut through and make firm and plain and smooth, straight paths for your feet [yes, make them safe and upright and happy paths that go in the right direction], so that the lame and halting [limbs] may not be put out of joint, but rather may be cured."
—Hebrews 12:13 AMP

Thomas Edison said that success is 10% inspiration and 90% perspiration. Completing a book requires consistent, dedicated effort based on a routine writing schedule. Just as road builders described in Hebrews 12:13 must apply themselves to diligent hard work through careful planning to ensure safe passage to travelers, so must writers be prepared to devote a significant part of their lives to developing a book that will guide readers through a clear-cut, meaningful message.

When God released the Israelites from Egyptian bondage under Moses' leadership, their journey to the Promised Land could have been completed in less than two weeks. But because they chose to disobey God, the trip dissolved into 40 years of desert wanderings:

"I have led you forty years in the wilderness; your clothes have not worn out upon you, and your sandals have not worn off your feet."
—Deuteronomy 29:5 AMP

Yet, God gave Moses the Ten Commandments in 40 days:

Moses was there with the Lord forty days and forty nights; he ate no bread and drank no water. And he wrote upon the tables the words of the covenant, the Ten Commandments."
—Exodus 34:28 AMP

Effective communication in adherence to God's standards can be speedily accomplished.

The number one reason why aspiring authors fail to get published is because they do not finish writing their manuscripts. It's easy to talk about writing a book. It's a little challenging to actually make an outline and get started. But it's hardest of all to stick to the task and produce a finished book within a set period of time. Sheer discipline is an absolute necessity; such work is not for procrastinators. Yet, thousands of books are published each year, and millions line library and bookstore shelves throughout the world, proof that many authors from ages past and present resisted the urge to quit and motivated themselves to keep on writing until their book was complete and ready for a publisher's review.

"And Peter opened his mouth and said: Most certainly and thoroughly I now perceive and understand that God shows no partiality and is no respecter of persons."
—Acts 10:34 AMP

Run for the Prize

No one knows if their book, when published, will be successful. We all hope so! And we trust that God is in control with a plan that includes your book's destiny. Your first goal as an author is to complete the charge that has been given to you: get the book written. There are plenty of possible obstacles to keep it from happening, but just as a marathon runner learns to watch for and avoid possible barriers in his path, so, also, must a writer prepare for daily distractions and unexpected emergencies that can bring creative momentum to a screeching halt, or perhaps a spiritual assault from the enemy himself, which we need not fear when we trust in God's provision:

"Who shall ever separate us from Christ's love? Shall suffering and affliction and tribulation? Or calamity and distress? Or persecution or hunger or destitution or peril or sword?"
—*Romans 8:35 AMP*

That's why, at the beginning of this book, you were advised to establish a 12-week plan that would let you work on your manuscript each day, or most days, at times when you are least likely to be interrupted. There was also the suggestion to let family members and friends know of your book project, or at least your new off-limits schedule times that would reduce or eliminate the number of phone calls or visits that might otherwise take place.

Now that you are several weeks into your writing plan, how is it going? Are you still on target, producing a chapter each week, so that you will finish up your manuscript within 90 days from the starting date? If not, what went wrong? Like a well-meaning dieter that gradually falls away from a sensible eating plan, have you strayed further and further from your purpose, leaving a blank computer screen sitting on your desk? Or have you been called away from your project by the television or a lack of focus? Remember Jesus' admonition about putting a hand to the plow and then looking back, or the tragedy of Lot's wife when she disobeyed and looked back on what she had left behind!

Staying faithful isn't easy. But if God has called you to the ministry of authoring a book, He will walk with you every step of the way. Whenever you feel discouraged or inadequate for the task of reaching the finish line, pray for the Heavenly Father's guidance and strength. There may be times when you're ready to give up. But wait—take a timeout first and bind the enemy. Sometimes a short respite is enough to refuel your energy and creativity, and get you back to work.

For we are glad when we are weak (unapproved) and you are really strong. And this we also pray for: your all-round strengthening and perfecting of soul."
—*II Corinthians 13:9 AMP*

Apply Biblical Principles You Have Learned

Don't wait to slide into the slumps while writing your book, and then totally abandon it while in the grip of despair. Call to mind all that you have been taught to apply during dry spiritual periods, tempestuous temptations, or creative exhaustion. Here are biblical proactive tips to practice when you feel as though your book has nowhere to go.

1. Seek God's voice when your own runs dry.

"If you have anything to say, answer me; speak, for I desire to justify you."

—(Job 33:32 AMP

Although you may feel as though you have nothing left to write about, go to God in prayer and ask His will. It may be He wants to add special meaning to your ideas when you contemplate them with Him. Find out if there is something you're supposed to learn, do, or see before continuing on with the book. God supplies all our needs through His strength when ours dwindles or disappears.

2. Humble yourself and admit that you need help.

"O Lord, You have heard the desire and the longing of the humble and oppressed; You will prepare and strengthen and direct their hearts, You will cause your ear to hear."

—Psalm 10:17 AMP

If you began the book with a passionate plan, you may feel frustrated and disappointed if the plan appears to halt or fall through. Then it might be tempting to hide your feeling of failure from others, so you make excuses about why you haven't finished your book. But when you admit defeat and helplessness, our Heavenly Father is gracious to step in and provides the direction we need to stay the course.

3. Choose to be happy and content, even when progress is slow.

"The path of the wise leads upward to life, that he may avoid [the gloom] in the depths of Sheol (Hades, the place of the dead).
[Phil. 3:20; Col. 3:1, 2.]"

—Proverbs 15:24 AMP

Going around with a bad attitude isn't going to get the book written or help you feel better, and it certainly isn't going to please God. Remember that you are the child of a King, and when your project stalls out, rejoice in the fact that your relationship with God is permanent—it can't fall through, deteriorate, or break. Be patient; inspiration will return.

4. Take a mental breather and set your writing aside temporarily.

"Cast Your bread upon the waters, for you will find it after many days."
—Ecclesiastes 11:1 AMP

It's possible that writing a book in 12 weeks may tax an over-burdened schedule to the point that you feel like quitting. Don't do it! Listen for God's voice by stopping work on the book and thinking about other things. In a day or two, come back to your writing project and see if it doesn't flow more smoothly.

5. Resist temptation to substitute other activities for writing time.

"And when He came to the place, He said to them, Pray that you may not [at all] enter into temptation."
—Luke 22:40 AMP

No matter the season, you're bound to feel the call of nature to enjoy the great outdoors after work or on weekends—probably during your writing sessions. You may feel the lure of seasonal sports viewing or participation, and you might want to clean out the garage or go shopping. Those activities are fine as long as they don't interfere with your writing time. Stay true to your purpose, and don't be lured from the track of success.

6. Remember to produce fruit for God's glory.

"When you bear (produce) much fruit, My Father is honored and glorified, and you show and prove your-selves to be true followers of Mine."
—John 15:8 AMP

While writing your book, no matter which plan you began with, you might get sidetracked into writing about something that matters to you, which may be related to the original topic, but still off course. Every Christian author's goal should strive to fulfill God's purpose for him or her in producing a piece of writing for publication. Check your work to be sure it glorifies God and has the potential to impact others for Christ. If not, revision will be needed to get you back on track.

7. Live peaceably with everyone so God can bless your work.

"He who exhorts (encourages), to his exhortation; he who contributes, let him do it in simplicity and liberality; he who gives aid and superintends, with zeal and single-ness of mind; he who does acts of mercy, with genuine cheerfulness and joyful eagerness."

—Romans 12:8 AMP

If you are having conflicts with loved ones, neighbors, or coworkers, chances are your writing will be affected. Get your personal life in order and arrange it hierarchically according to Scriptural mandates: God first, spouse and family second, job third, and so on. If you are struggling with anger, depression, or another negative emotion based on relationship issues, make peace with the people involved so you can move on with your ministry.

8. Write as though competing for a prize (you are!).

"Do you not know that in a race all the runners compete, but [only] one receives the prize? So run [your race] that you may lay hold [of the prize] and make it yours."

—I Corinthians 9:24 AMP

Remember riding the merry-go-round and reaching for the brass ring? It took every ounce of self-control and muscle coor-dination to stretch out and grasp the prize without losing your balance. No matter how many times you missed the ring, you would keep on trying as long as possible to try and get it. That's how you should feel about your book. The stakes are much higher now, with eternal consequences as the "prize" or "punishment" to those on board. Don't give up! Keep at it until you accomplish what you set out to do.

9. Double-check your motives.

"Do nothing from factional motives [through conten-tiousness, strife, selfishness, or for unworthy ends] or prompted by conceit and empty arrogance. Instead, in the true spirit of humility (lowliness of mind) let each regard the others as better than and superior to himself [thinking more highly of one another than you do of yourselves]."
—Philippians 2:3 AMP

Are you writing this book for ministry or money? There's nothing wrong with earning income from your writing work, but if that is your primary goal, you should re-think your priorities. A pure heart is essential for authoring a book God's way. If you are writing from impure motives, it's time to set your project aside and get in touch with God.

10. Avoid immature temptations and pursue righteous desires.

"Shun youthful lusts and flee from them, and aim at and pursue righteousness (all that is virtuous and good, right living, conformity to the will of God in thought, word, and deed); [and aim at and pursue] faith, love, [and] peace (harmony and concord with others) in fellowship with all (Christians), who call upon the Lord out of a pure heart."
—II Timothy 2:22-23 AMP

A new television series, a bowling league, or the opportunity to work overtime may compete with your desire to write a book for God's glory. All of these things are great pastimes, but which will better further the Kingdom? If you are in doubt, commune with God to find out if you should be writing a book at this time in your life. Maybe you have misunderstood the plan, or perhaps you need to put the book on hold for now.

"[For being as he is] a man of two minds (hesitating, dubious, irresolute, [he is] unstable and unreliable and uncertain about everything [he thinks, feels, decides]."
—James 1:8 AMP

Many things in this world can hold us back from meeting goals and serving God. That's why it is important to test your faith if you find yourself unable to continue writing. It may be that your attention is being diverted to worldly distractions. Or perhaps God would like a word with you about new or changed plans for the book.

No matter the reason, deal with it promptly. Then return to your original writing schedule (unless God directs you otherwise) and continue the work per your plan. As you complete each chapter, make sure it is fully developed and explains the main idea being presented. Then set that section aside while you move on to write the next chapter. Eventually, you will return to your first draft and review each chapter closely, making revisions and edits that will improve it. For now, your task is to get ideas in print where they will be easier to work with. Staying focused and completing this part of the book-writing plan will help to fulfill your ministry commitment and keep you from getting bogged down in senseless delays.

"And I sent messengers to them, saying, I am doing a great work and cannot come down. Why should the work stop while I leave to come down to you?"
—Nehemiah 6:3 AMP

Writer's Wisdom:
Am I dealing responsibly with obstacles to my 90-day writing plan?

For Revelation:
"I press on toward the goal to win the [supreme and heavenly] prize to which God in Christ Jesus is calling us upward."
—Philippians 3:14 AMP

In today's fast-paced society, it's hard to keep going when you feel the pull of other duties or become distracted from completing the book. But if you keep going, God will bless your efforts, as long as He is involved with the project from start to finish.

The Master's Writing Plan Activities
Writing Step #1:

Make a list of actual distractions that have interfered with your writing the book. One by one, deal with each of them after praying about them. Keep track of their disposition so you can be sure they are addressed.

Writing Step #2:

Now list possible distractions that may pop up over the next several weeks. (These might be related to holidays, birthdays, work schedule, home repairs, etc.). Write a few sentences to explain how you will manage them to prevent their interference with your writing.

Writing Step #3:

If you are experiencing a stop-and-start effect in your writing, make a weekly schedule that allocates adequate time for keeping your book on schedule. Use a check-mark beside each writing session and/or date to show visual progress on your book.

New Testament Reading Plan Week #8:

Acts 27 through I Corinthians 4

Chapter Nine:

Streams in the Desert

"Then shall the lame man leap like a hart,
And the tongue of the dumb shall sing for joy.
For waters shall break forth in the wilderness and streams in the desert.
[Matt. 11:5]"
—Isaiah 35:6 AMP

Welcome to Week Nine!

If you've been writing your book for eight weeks now, you may be feeling anxious and discouraged, like someone who has wandered in the desert and isn't sure which way to go. Recall how the children of Israel wandered in their desert of disobedience for 40 years, until God finally allowed them to enter the Promised Land, as described in the Book of Exodus. Their prolonged journey sprang from the refusal to trust God for every detail of their survival, including the need for drinkable water in a parched, arid region. God delivered them, according to His purpose and promise, although He took His time in fulfilling that promise when His people failed to keep their faith centered on God.

Your journey through the book you are writing may seem endless. In fact, you might feel like giving up, just as the Israelites clamored to return to Egypt. But you can't look back now! You must complete your quest to craft the message with which you have been entrusted. If you are somewhat uncertain about how to proceed, push yourself to write a certain number of words or pages each day. One typed, double-spaced page averages about 200 words. A chapter of ten pages would total about 2,000 words. Twenty chapters will represent 40,000 words, which is about the size of a non-fiction book or one-half the size of a typical novel. If you can write five pages per day, you will have 1,000 words. At the end of 30 days, you will have written 30,000 words, and in 90 days, 90,000 words—a perfectly-sized work of fiction.

Whether fiction or non-fiction, you must keep on writing until your message has been produced. I believe it is possible for you to manifest this message in 90 days, according to this book's plan. But you have to stay focused and keep writing a little on most days. If you stop, you may never start writing again. Don't give up now!

If you continue writing by following this 90-day plan, soon you will have a complete manuscript. It will be challenging. You may need to take out some parts and rewrite others. It might need further explanation and detail to be clear for readers. When you have at least 40,000 words in print, or 200 double-spaced pages of non-fiction or 300 double-spaced pages of fiction, and if you feel your basic message has been captured in the draft, you are ready to begin the revising process. Revising encompasses many aspects of improvement, such as review, editing, rewriting, and proof-reading your manuscript.

What is Revision?

Revision means "seeing again" (re-vision). It means you go back over what you have written and look for ways to make it better, stronger, and clearer. This comprehensive review gives you the opportunity of accomplishing the following essential tasks:

Revising:

The Bible calls Christians to be good stewards over their lands and belongings. The same principle applies to our intellectual property. It is important for Christian authors to do the best possible job with book manuscripts, as their work ultimately becomes a testimony to their relationship with the Lord.

"A man's gift makes room for him and brings him before great men. [Gen. 32:20, I Sam. 25:27, Prov. 17:8; 21:14.]"
—Proverbs 18:16 AMP

Look over the entire manuscript to be sure the message or story is fully developed. Check to be sure your book follows the conventions of its genre, that is, non-fiction should adhere to industry guidelines for factual or experiential information. Fiction should be structured according to the type of story being told, whether a historical romance, contemporary suspense, or action thriller. You will want to review the following as you make your way through the manuscript:

1. Structure.

Does each chapter follow the same format? For example, have you set the chapter titles in the same type size and font? Are they spaced similarly—for example, about 12 lines from the top of the chapter's first page? (Succeeding pages can begin higher on the page, but the title heading usually is placed a little lower, and in larger font size, perhaps bolded, to make it stand out and grab readers' attention.)

Double space all lines, at least when you finish the manuscript, to make it readable for editors, reviewers, publishers, etc. Check pagination for accuracy and consistency. Your chapters should be roughly uniform in length within a few pages, for example, between five and eight pages each, or whatever length you prefer.

If you are adding Scripture, verses, or chapter-end activities or exercises, are these structured the same way in terms of font, arrangement, and placement? All chapters from beginning to end should appear more or less uniform in headings, section organization, font, and style.

Have you created a Table of Contents with appropriate page numbers? Do you have a Notes page at the end and/or a Works Cited page (if needed)? How about an index? A writing expert can help you prepare these materials, if you are unsure about how to do them on your own.

2. Development.

Review your book's main premise, which should be described and explained in the Preface, Note to Readers, Introduction, or first chapter. Underline or bold this section to make your purpose stand out. Is it the same idea you started with? If so, you will want to check chapter headings to make sure they link back to the thesis at the beginning, and develop part of the premise in each chapter. Look for similar or related ideas between the beginning of your book and each subsequent chapter.

If the book seems to veer off track at some point and begins to discuss a different idea (goes off on a tangent), you will need to revise that section to get it to line up with the original idea. This could happen in random areas of one or more chapters, or you might find it throughout the rest of the book. Hopefully not! But if so, continue to rewrite those sections until the manuscript becomes a seamless unfolding of your ideas that connect to each other from beginning to end, each building on a previous idea to add to new revelation that expands on the basic idea already in place.

3. Clarity.

Read through one chapter at a time, mindfully considering the way it is written and what it says, as well as how you've said it. Is the main idea clear and easy to understand? Or do you have trouble discerning the key point(s) of the chapter? Here are a few ways to check your writing style to ensure it is clear:

1   Simple vocabulary. Keep language basic but descriptive.
2   Logic. Do the ideas make sense? Are they persuasive and informative?
3   Focus. Does the book flow from a Christ-centered, clearly-stated idea?

As an author, one of your tasks is to make reading your book as easy as possible. Make sure that each chapter invites readers to continue reading through challenging ideas or insightful views.

"The sower sows the Word."
—Mark 4:14 AMP

4. Style.

Your personal writing style is made up of many different components. These usually vary from one author to another, but it is good to be aware of your style so you can make it serve your purposes in every writing project. Here are some things to be aware of:

118

1   Tone. What type of mood does the book use—informative, humorous, reflective?

2   Person. Are you writing in first person (I, me, my, mine) or third person (him, her, a person, etc.)? Which will be more effective for this book? If you stick with first person, don't overuse "I" or the book will seem writer-centered rather than reader-centered.

3   Verb tense. Are you using mostly present tense or past tense? Why? Whatever you use, keep verb tenses consistent; avoid switching between past and present.

4   Voice. Are you using active voice or passive voice? Generally, active voice is preferable, as it is more direct and less wordy: The car hit the dog. (Passive: The dog was hit by the car.)

5   Sentence complexity. Use a variety of simple, compound, and complex sentences.

5. Induction.

What a message says and what it means are a reader's chief concerns. The third is how to apply insight gleaned from these observations to your life. If you haven't already, this is an excellent approach to personal Bible study. Then, as you write your book, it is important to encourage readers to apply the same principles.

"In it I became a minister in accordance with the divine stewardship which was entrusted to me for you [as its object and for your benefit], to make the Word of God fully known [among you]—
The mystery of which was hidden for ages and generations [from angels and men], but is now revealed to His holy people (the saints),"
—Colossians 1:25-26 AMP

Let's say that you want your book to help readers use an inductive approach to Bible study. You would first make sure you have used this method, understand it, and can explain it to others. Then you would break down the process into small, manageable units of information or advice that readers could easily grasp and begin to use. You might use an approach similar to this:

1   Read the Scripture passage for general understanding. Look up words or meanings you don't know.

2   Think about the passage's literal and universal meanings. Could some words be symbolic? Does the message apply to a set point in time or does it include readers today?

3   Decide how this passage of Scripture can enhance your understanding of God's truths and be viewed as practical advice for Christian life today.

Writing about a concept with which you have experience and in which you believe makes it more interesting and useful to readers.

6.   Check research.

If you are citing facts, statistics, or interviews in your book, be sure to double- and triple-check your sources for up-to-date information and correct citations. Few errors invalidate an author's credibility more quickly than weak or careless research and citations. Use a consistent documentation style, like the Chicago Manual of Style, depending on your book's topic. (Humanities topics use the Modern Language Association—MLA—style of documentation, while social sciences uses the American Psychological Association—APA—style. There are several others, as well.)

In learning to revise, or "re-see" your writing again after completing your manuscript, you are giving yourself a second chance to rewrite it even better in the second and subsequent rounds. Take your time, read slowly and thoughtfully, and you are sure to catch things you missed while writing. Now is the time to review the work with an eye to making it even better before sending your manuscript to an agent or publisher.

Editing:

One Biblical principle that might be applied to editing is the concept of cleaning up our mistakes and giving our best to God. Just as David poured out his heart to God in Psalm 51 after his sin in attempting to make things right with God, so should authors use the revision and editing process to catch mistakes and improve their work. After all, a published book becomes a print testimony to an author's beliefs and practices. Here are some things to look for as you consider editing your work, after completing the larger task of revising the manuscript.

1   Examine the order and organization of your writing. Does anything need to be expanded, shrunk, added, or omitted? Do you need to move any paragraphs around or even reorganize some of the chapters? If so, this is the time to do it. You might need to lengthen a section or add another one.

2   Does each chapter have its own topic that is well developed with adequate examples? If not, insert explanations, evidence, or charts to clarify main ideas.

3   Can the writing be tighter? Can you eliminate extra, unnecessary words or phrases? (Ex: It has often been thought = People often think)

4   Have you repeated ideas or words? Repetition for emphasis can be good, as demonstrated in the Ten Commandments' repetition of "Thou shalt not" or "Thou shalt," for consistency. Careless repetition, on the other hand, should be avoided.

5   Does your intro clearly lead into the main idea? Does it grab readers' attention? Can you think of a hook to add in the first paragraph or two?

6   Does the conclusion neatly summarize the main idea? Does it leave readers with a profound revelation or principle to think about and possibly adopt in their lives? Does it restate the main points?

Don't be hesitant to edit your work by changing or rearranging information. If you don't do it now to improve the manuscript, chances are an agent or publisher will insist on it later—if your book gets that far. Give your manuscript every chance to succeed by being brutally honest and scrupulously diligent in making effective changes that will enhance the final product. Apply the old grammar adage: "When in doubt, leave it out."

Polishing:
Remember how great it feels to drive your car just after it's been washed? Whether you hand-washed it yourself or drove through an auto-

matic carwash, you undoubtedly love the feeling of driving a clean, bright vehicle still sparkling with fresh drops of clean water.

Now recall how it felt when you went a step further and got the car waxed. Maybe you applied it or got it done in the automatic carwash. Wasn't it a terrific feeling to drive that car around, all polished as though it were new again, feeling good in knowing that your vehicle looked its best? As an individual vehicle owner, there wasn't much more you could do to bring out your car's best features for others to notice.

The same can be true of your writing. By taking time to revise and edit, you are "cleaning" the manuscript to make it correct and neat. In adding the extra step of "polishing," you can take an adequate manuscript and make it absolutely brilliant! Here are a few hints to keep in mind as you finalize your book for publication:

1. **Figurative language.** Can you gracefully add metaphors, similes, or alliteration to your writing style without their seeming out of place or ostentatious? How about personification or an analogy? A sentence or two of these devices, or a paragraph at most, can do much to improve the quality and interest of your writing style and enhance its readability.

2. **Diction.** Without going overboard, can you find exciting substitutions for some of your word choices or expressions? Avoid clichés, but instead, create your own innovative statements that will linger in readers' minds afterward. Avoid archaic, technical, or overly sentimental writing. Rely on crisp words to convey an idea.

3. **Catchy quotes.** You can add a song lyric or poem's line (with permission from the publishing company), a folk saying, a proverb, a definition, or another type of special language use, often beneath the chapter title or to open a chapter as a first line, to get readers' attention and make them start thinking. The Old Testament Book of Genesis begins with the phrase, "In the beginning...." as does the New Testament Book of John. So there is continuity between the two covenants. Can you establish similar linkages between parts of your book without sounding repetitious?

4. **Create an eye- or ear-grabbing title.** You can do this both for the book overall and for each chapter to ensure that readers continue

to move readily from one chapter to the next until they finish the book. Alliteration or rhyme can achieve this effect.

5   **Clarify your purpose.** Although this really should be managed in the revising or editing process, you can focus on it here to make your purpose obvious to readers. It can be stated in your book's first paragraph and perhaps restated in slightly different phrasing in the final paragraph. Or it can be developed a little more in each chapter as readers become more familiar with your ideas. Just make sure both your readers and you know what your purpose is.

After completing these activities, you should feel much more confident about your finished manuscript. Now you are almost ready to finalize your book for publication. You may even want to go through the manuscript another time or two to look for errors you missed. Keep an open mind about the need to find weaknesses and correct them. No one is perfect, and your manuscript very likely will need, and benefit from, quality review. As you work through the final stages of completing your manuscript, trust that God will be with you, guiding and inspiring you each step of the way. Seek His courage and strength if your creativity begins to fade—you're almost there!

Writer's Wisdom:
Which parts of my book need to be rewritten or polished to have a greater impact for the advancement of the Kingdom?

For Revelation:
"And I am convinced and sure of this very thing, that He Who began a good work in you will continue until the day of Jesus Christ [right up to the time of His return], developing [that good work] and perfecting and bringing it to full completion in you."
—Philippians 1:6 AMP

The Master's Writing Plan Activities
Writing Step #1:
Follow the revising guidelines described in this chapter. Write a couple of sentences describing the changes that are made from the original manuscript.

Writing Step #2:

Now go through the editing process, making sure to review each chapter with an eye for the overall picture as well as the intricate details. Again, write a summary sentence or two explaining some of the changes you've made in this part of the process.

Writing Step #3:

Reflect on the polishing step of your manuscript. Briefly describe any improvements you are able to make that will help your writing to shine more brightly than ever before in a way that will bring glory to God.

New Testament Reading Plan Week #9:

I Corinthians 5 through Galatians 6

Chapter Ten

Run the Race!

"Therefore Then, since we are surrounded by so great a cloud of
witnesses [who have borne testimony to the Truth], let us strip off and
throw aside every encumbrance (unnecessary weight) and that sin which
so readily (deftly and cleverly) clings to and entangles us, and let us run
with patience endurance and steady and active persistence the appointed
course of the race that is set before us,"
—Hebrews 12:1 AMP

At last, you've finished the manuscript. Your message is fully explained in the pages of your soon-to-be-published book. You've reviewed each chapter extensively, and even sought feedback from others. Your fingers relax. Your task is complete.

But your work is not done. Just as God's preparation of the children of Israel for the Promised Land required forty years of desert wandering, and David waited seven years to assume the rule of Israel, so it is with many good works. It's true that some ministries can achieve great things very quickly, sometimes in a matter of moments or hours, as during an altar call or a witnessing opportunity. Choice words may take immediate effect, like well-deserved praise or a deserved rebuke.

But your book, when printed and published, will be around for a long time. Because of its lasting value, you want to give it your best efforts to represent a biblical perspective and a professional style. Now is your chance to review what you've written to be sure your ideas are expressed clearly and accurately for the readers whose lives will be impacted. Don't take this opportunity lightly to review, revise, and polish your work to make it gleam with meaning and glow with hope. Check to make sure that your message is crystal-clear and inviting to those who will read it:

> *"And let your instruction be sound and fit and wise and whole-some, vigorous and irrefutable and above censure, so that the opponent may be put to shame, finding nothing discrediting or evil to say about us."*
> —*Titus 2:8 AMP*

Do a Thorough Self-Review

In an earlier chapter, you were advised to check your manuscript for important things that will help to ensure it develops as it should. After all, your goal as a Christian author is to share Biblical truths with your readers, so your message must be clear, scriptural, and consistent. While writing each chapter these past several weeks, you eagerly formed words to frame your ideas and wrote sentence after sentence to describe them. Now that you are nearing the completion of your manuscript, it's time to prepare for self-editing, a challenging and vital part of the writing process.

As soon as you finish that last chapter, set your book aside for a few days—as many as you can spare on the 90-day writing schedule, in fact. This might end up being two or three days for some, and a week or more for others. Getting away from your writing will give you time to reflect on your message and the way it is written. More importantly, you will be able to forget about it temporarily and focus on other tasks or interests. Then, when it's time, you will return to your manuscript with a "fresh eye" for reviewing what you've written and making necessary changes, corrections, and improvements, as well as aligning your ideas with Biblical principles.

> *"And God purposed that through (by the service, the intervention of) Him [the Son] all things should be completely reconciled back to Himself, whether on earth or in heaven, as through Him, [the Father] made peace by means of the blood of His cross."*
> —*Colossians 1:20*

If you are still not finished writing your book, continue to compose a chapter each week, per the original schedule. But take time this week to go back to chapters one through four to begin the process of evalu-ating and strengthening what you have done so far. Next week, you will review chapters five through eight, and in week twelve, as your project finishes up, you will be ready to review chapters nine through twelve and to prepare the entire manuscript for publication.

What should you look for in revising your writing? Just as you did earlier in the project, you will read through the first several chapters in search of ways to make it better. Here is a basic checklist of what to do.

1. Do chapters have topics that link to the book's overall theme?

Look for the main idea of each chapter somewhere near the begin-ning, perhaps in the first paragraph or two. Readers should know very quickly what this chapter will do, and how it connects to the rest of the book. If this is not readily apparent as you go over it now, rewrite the chapter's introduction to clarify the focus. Make sure you don't have any ill-fitting chapters that seem to branch off on a tangent idea that doesn't really fit with the rest of the book. If you find a chapter that seems to do this, try to rewrite it for a better fit, or consider dropping it from the book.

2. Is each chapter fully and Biblically developed?

Do you see extra short or very long chapters that seem out of balance with the others? Do any of the chapters read in a vague way, as though going in circles or hinting at something without explaining it? These are the development aspects of your writing style that you will want to catch now and fix before publishing the book for others to read. While the chapters don't have to be perfectly uniform and have the exact number of pages, they should be relatively similar, for example, having perhaps between ten and fifteen pages each. A chapter with five pages or one with twenty-two might need to be adjusted for enhanced flow.

3. Are your ideas adequately explained and logically supported?

In reading through each chapter, does it seem as though the main topic is easy to understand? Have you provided adequate support from research or case studies that are up-to-date, say, no earlier than ten years ago? Is your logic flawed or flawless? Have you considered opposing viewpoints to show readers you've done your homework and remain convinced of your book's position? Do you quote Biblical passages? Have you done so accurately, using the appropriate translation?

4. Does the writing have a thoughtful or engaging tone?

Will your style of writing make readers want to continue through the book, or does it seem empty of true feelings and perhaps light on meaning? Are you limiting your use of first person (I, we, my) and second person (you, yours)? There's nothing wrong with using the personalized voice, but don't overdo it. A general rule of thumb that really is flexible is to avoid starting your paragraphs with a reference to the author ("I," "My," etc.). Instead, begin paragraphs with references to the message or the reader. Try not to use "I" too often throughout.

Likewise, use phrasing that will attract readers to Scripture and want to learn more about a personal relationship with the Lord Jesus Christ, while gently correcting false impressions of Christianity through the help of the Holy Spirit.

"He must correct his opponents with courtesy and gentleness, in the hope that God may grant that they will repent and come to know the Truth [that they will perceive and recognize and become accurately acquainted with and acknowledge it],"
—II Timothy 2:25 AMP

5. Reinforce action verbs and concrete nouns.

Look for use of "to be" and "to have" verbs, including past, present, and future usage, as well as others, like the conditional tense. You may want to print off a copy of the chapter and circle all of these uses. Then consider replacing words like these with stronger words. For example:

Not this: "Being popular is very important to teens."
Try this: "Popularity is very important to teens."

Do the same for weak nouns or pronouns.

Not this: "Many people witnessed the bridge collapse."
But this: "Many drivers and pedestrians witnessed the bridge collapse."

Continually look for ways to enhance your explanations and descriptions. You don't have to use large or rare words to impress readers. Just choose those that are clear and colorful. Above all, let your spiritual message shine forth from your pages to encourage and inspire your readers:

"I know you are enduring patiently and are bearing up for My name's sake, and you have not fainted or become exhausted or grown weary."
—Revelation 2:3 AMP

Of course, you may need to move around some sentences or add a little more explanation in a few places. Just don't get carried away with excessive description or over-emphasizing ideas.

Seek Competent Feedback
When you have read each chapter thoroughly and made all the edits you can find, consider asking someone whose judgment you trust to read your work and share an opinion on its merit. This could be a former teacher, a colleague, a secretary, a friend, or even a family member, but hopefully it will be someone who can recognize the flaws in your writing and will point them out directly and politely. You can discuss the book over coffee or ask for email feedback so you can ponder the reader's response while you are alone before meeting that person face-to-face. Be appreciative of anyone willing to share his or her time to make your book all that it can be, even if they express concerns about some areas that could benefit from additional attention or revising.

You may want to consider getting professional feedback on your book. Sometimes called "coverage," this entails paying a professional writer, editor, or publisher to read your manuscript and send you a written report of one or several pages. The report might include suggestions for improvement, or it might just point out the weaknesses, but either way, you will have more information for improving your book, if the reader has worthwhile credentials that render his or her opinion valuable. Many book editing services can be found online. Evaluate them prayerfully to find someone who is well-trained and experienced in the art of writing.

Proofreading

Proofreading (also called "proofing") your writing can be done any number of ways. Assuming you have written your book on a computer's word processor, your composing program may have a spell-check function that will catch many errors for you. Always run this one or more times while in the revising stage of a writing project.

Never assume a spell-check feature will catch all mistakes, however. That's why you need to use other proofreading strategies, as well. One way is to read through each chapter very slowly, looking for misspellings, misuse of punctuation, or other surface errors. Another approach is to read the chapter backward, beginning at the end and reading one word at a time to get back to the beginning. The going will be slow, allowing you to find things that might otherwise be missed. A third option is to ask someone to read a copy of the chapter as you listen, and you may catch additional problems that way.

No matter how you do it, be sure to look over the entire chapter several times before pronouncing it "ready to publish." Setting it aside for a few days between readings will help you return to it more ready to find flaws and to correct weaknesses, and to strengthen the important Biblical truths that can guide readers' lives.

> *"[So] that in Him in every respect you were enriched, in full power and readiness of speech [to speak of your faith] and complete knowledge and illumination (to give you full insight into its meaning)."*
> *—I Corinthians 1:5 AMP*

Request Early Reviews

When you are fairly certain the book is completely polished and ready for self-publishing, that is the time to organize six to twelve bound copies of your manuscript, before it is officially bound and published, and ship them to reviewers who are willing to read the book and post their opinion on websites or in print publications, like journals or magazines. Sometimes newspapers and newsletters will publish book reviews, as well.

Do an online search for book reviewers in your manuscript's genre, i.e., "self-help book reviewers." Contact those you think would be interested, and ask them to review your bound copy, called a "galley." Explain where you are at in the publishing process, and if they agree, send a bound copy with the understanding you may never see it again. (It doesn't matter, as you will soon have published copies anyway.)

Keep in mind that a review can be negative as well as positive, and you'll have to live with the published evaluation that may be available to hundreds or thousands of readers. If you receive good reviews, you can use blurbs (or parts) of them as promotional pieces for your book's publication. Incorporate the positive opinions in press releases, cover blurbs, posters, etc. Amazon.com is a good place to have your book posted, along with any favorable reviews that it receives.

Writer's Wisdom:
What can I do to promote my book's ideas and obtain pre-publishing publicity?

For Revelation:
"Hear counsel, receive instruction, and accept correction that you may be wise in the time to come."
—Proverbs 19:20 AMP

The Master's Writing Plan Activities
Writing Step #1:
Review chapters one through four again with the goal of finalizing your ideas, revising your style, and improving your accuracy. Use a marker or pen on a print copy of the manuscript, or turn on your computer's word processing editor to track your changes. Try to find at least five things to correct or improve on each page, no matter how often you've done it before.

Writing Step #2:
Ask at least one other person to read your first four chapters. Specify the form in which you would like to receive feedback, i.e., written list of

errors, an email report, or an informal discussion. Be open to suggestions and even criticisms, knowing that they can help you view your work from a reader's perspective and make any necessary changes for improvement.

Writing Step #3:

Try a different proofreading technique than you have used before. See if it helps you find more mistakes, or different kinds, than you usually do. If the new technique doesn't seem especially effective, try another one next time.

New Testament Reading Plan Week #10:

Ephesians 1 through II Thessalonians.

Chapter Eleven

To the Glory of God

"Let the high praises of God be in their throats and a two-edged sword
in their hands.
[Heb. 4:12; Rev. 1:16]"
—Psalm 149:6 AMP

On the home stretch, you are ready for the final run-through of your soon-to-be-published book. Hopefully, in the near future, readers will be able to enjoy and benefit from the Godly wisdom you have shared on each page of your book. But before you send your spiritual offspring into the world to influence others, it is important to review and evaluate your work by comparing it to your original goal to be sure the book is headed in the right direction.

In Chapter Two, Master's Plan Step #1 directed you to write a mission statement for your book, along with a short one- or two-sentence description of each chapter to ensure your plan was cohesive and Biblically focused. Having done that, you then went on to write your book over the weeks that followed, arriving at this point in time with a complete or nearly finished manuscript that is being prepared for publication.

Now it's time to recheck your Christ-centered objectives to see if you were able to stay on track with the original plan. If you have veered in another direction, there's still time to get your ideas re-focused. Seek feedback from writers, teachers, or spiritual leaders whose opinion you trust:

"And let us consider and give attentive, continuous care to watching over one another, studying how we may stir up (stimulate and incite) to love and helpful deeds and noble activities"
—Hebrews 10:24 AMP

The Bible provides numerous examples of God's chosen people who began with His plan directing their lives, only to find themselves wandering off course and headed for trouble. Beginning with Adam and Eve and continuing through the Old Testament and into the New Testament, we can find many well-meaning followers of God who ended up on the wrong path through carelessness, temptation or sheer disobedience. Samson, Balaam, David, and Solomon began their ministries well, but somehow took a wrong turn that led to disaster. Fortunately, getting a little off focus with your book should not lead to death or destruction. Nevertheless, you want to do the best possible job with it as a ministry tool and a source of satisfaction.

Check Your Compass Direction
As with any journey, it's important to choose a sensible starting point. Presumably, you have done that by beginning your book with prayer and meditation. You also have chosen a support tool, in the form of this book, to guide your journey through the twelve-week writing path.

"Do you see a man diligent and skillful in his business? He will stand before kings; he will not stand before obscure men."
—Proverbs 22:29 AMP
"Your word is a lamp to my feet and a light to my path. [Prov. 6:23.]"
—Psalm 119:105 AMP

Through the help of periodic re-checks as coordinated in the Master's Plan writing steps at the end of each chapter, you have had the opportunity to review your progress and check back to your starting point to ensure consistency along the route. Now that you are at the end of your journey, it is important to once more return to the source of your plan and determine whether you have faithfully followed the map that you originally created.

"But be doers of the Word [obey the message], and not merely listeners to it, betraying yourselves [into deception by reasoning contrary to the Truth].

For if anyone only listens to the Word without obeying it and being a doer of it, he is like a man who looks carefully at his [own] natural face in a mirror:

For he thoughtfully observes himself, and then goes off and promptly forgets what he was like.

But he who looks carefully into the faultless law, the [law] of liberty, and is faithful to it and perseveres in looking into it, being not a heedless listener who forgets but an active doer [who obeys], he shall be blessed in his doing (his life of obedience)"
—James 1:22-25 AMP

The next part of this chapter will guide you through the self-check process. If you have deviated from your original plan, decide whether you need to amend the preliminary outline that began the book, or if it would be better to adjust any of the chapters that might be pulling away from the initial outline. Hopefully your authorship journey has led upward toward the high calling of Christ, and perhaps you now find yourself on an elevated Christ-centered plane:

"But you, beloved, build yourselves up [founded] on your most holy faith [make progress, rise like an edifice higher and higher]. praying in the Holy Spirit;"
—Jude 1:20 AMP

Don't be concerned if you have strayed from the preliminary concept that got the book going. Sometimes we say that we "write to learn" as much as we "learn to write." In other words, you may be learning more about your topic as you develop each chapter, so it would not be unusual for your perspective to change somewhat as you work through the book and arrive at the conclusion. Now you just have to line up the focus with the outcomes to ensure that everything is consistent from start to finish, and that the book unfolds spiritually and graciously to reveal key Biblical insights to help readers mature in God.

At this level of assessment, you must first reflect on the ways in which writing your book has impacted your relationship with God. You also need to be aware of the implications and opportunities for leadership that very possibly may come your way, and consequently, be prepared for them with both confidence and humility.

> *"Him we preach and proclaim, warning and admonishing everyone and instructing everyone in all wisdom (comprehensive insight into the ways and purposes of God), that we may present every person mature (full-grown, fully initiated, complete and perfect) in Christ (the Anointed One)."*
> *—Colossians 1:28 AMP*

How the Book Has Changed You?

When you began planning your book, you had a spiritual mission in mind. It might have entailed personal growth, evangelistic outreach, or ministry support, along with a host of other options. Perhaps the project grew out of a very special time of closeness with God, or conversely, from a dry spiritual valley in which you were struggling. But remember that either way, you have been chosen for this special mission:

> *"For many are called (invited and summoned), but few are chosen."*
> *—Matthew 22:14 AMP*

Whatever the reason, your book reflects an important part of your spiritual being and your relationship with God. Readers should be able to see images of the Almighty in your words, and perhaps glimpses of themselves as well. By setting a publishing ministry goal, you have taken a leadership stand with the book to help others. Perhaps those objectives of impacting others for Christ were more implicit than explicit at first. But now, as you reach the end of your goal in completing the manuscript, you will want to check and see if your book fulfills its intended purpose and is likely to influence others to think, feel, or behave in a more Christ-like way. Here are some questions to ask yourself as you reflect on your book's overall purpose:

136

1. What was your relationship with the Father like before you wrote the book?
2. How has writing this book affected your relationship with Him? Has your life changed in visible ways, to others, as a result?
3. Do you view your book's purpose now as you did at the beginning? If not, how do you see it differently at this point?

Although you may have written your book with the primary view of assisting others with spiritual dilemmas or providing a Christian-based perspective on contemporary issues from everyday life, the experience undoubtedly has left its mark on you. Try to understand what that is before you proceed to the next step of reflection. Very likely, you are a different person today than you were a few months ago. Hopefully, you are walking more closely with the Lord than ever before, and your book will evidence that relationship. As a Christian author, you have assumed a position of spiritual leadership that readers are bound to acknowledge. You may find that upon your book's publication, you will be invited to speak at various events or to certain organizations. Writing your book has helped you complete a spiritual journey that will lift you to a platform of prominence. More than ever, you must guard your witness and be prepared to share your faith in relevant ways, depending on the group with which you may be interacting.

"For it is not you who are speaking, but the Spirit of your Father speaking through you."
—Matthew 10:20 AMP

How the Book Can Impact Readers
After realizing the types of changes that you could be experiencing as a result of this project, give some thought to how the book might influence those that read it. You began the book with a spiritual purpose in mind; did you finish it with the same purpose having been met?

Below are several criteria to consider when evaluating your book's effectiveness. Of course, it's hard to say how anyone will think or feel after reading it. Your audience of readers may be large and diverse. Some may be more spiritually grounded than others. But overall, you may want to have a life-changing impact that will enhance the reader's relationship with God and improve his or her testimony or ministry. While you can't guarantee these things will happen, by faith and prayer you can still do everything in your power to influence others through the printed word until it leaves your hands as a printed volume.

> *"For this reason I am telling you, whatever you ask for in prayer, believe (trust and be confident) that it is granted to you, and you will [get it]."*
> *—Mark 11:24 AMP*
>
> *"Is anyone among you sick? He should call in the church elders (the spiritual guides). And they should pray over him, anointing him with oil in the Lord's name.*
>
> *And the prayer [that is] of faith will save him who is sick, and the Lord will restore him; and if he has committed sins, he will be forgiven."*
> *—James 5:14-15 AMP*

As you conduct the following evaluations, keep in mind that no human handiwork is perfect. We do our best and leave the rest to God. As you complete your book, continue to pray for God's favor and His guidance in your publishing and marketing efforts, not for self-enrichment or popularity, but to ensure the book reaches those who need to read it most. Then be willing to follow God's commands:

> *"If any man has ears to hear, let him be listening and let him perceive and comprehend."*
> *—Mark 4:23 AMP*

Compare the Beginning with the End
When you finally write that last chapter and have gone through the final three chapters one more time to review and correct that material, you will be finished, more or less. Give yourself a day or two to let ideas settle, and to take a break from everything you have written. Then do the following:

1. Write a brief summary of the book's main idea as you wrote it, the way you remember it, now that you have been done for a few days.

2. Now skim through the entire book, checking chapter headings, to refresh your memory about what was actually written. Jot down a few sentences that summarize what is actually there, not what you recall (as you did in item #1 above).

3. Finally, go back to Chapter Two and re-read your summary idea for Writing Step #2. Compare what you wrote then with the summaries you have just completed now. Look for connected links between the chapters as well as between the beginning and end of the book. If you find broken links, decide how to repair or replace them.

In comparing your original idea with the final manuscript, you will be able to see how closely you followed the Master's Writing Plan. If you find relatively small deviations that are manageable, go ahead and adjust them, staying on target with this book to finish your manuscript in the twelve-week structure. But if you identify strategic problems requiring more extensive revision, you will need to take time to do a good job of fixing these before attempting to publish your book. Don't worry if you cannot complete the process in twelve weeks. You have done a remarkable job in getting this far along so quickly. Finishing the project in a little more time should not be a problem.

> *"And let us not lose heart and grow weary and faint in acting nobly and doing right, for in due time and at the appointed season we shall reap, if we do not loosen and relax our courage and faint."*
> *—Galatians 6:9 AMP*
> *"Therefore, Since we do hold and engage in this ministry by the mercy of God [granting us favor, benefits, opportunities, and especially salvation], we do not get discouraged (spiritless and despondent with fear) or become faint with weariness and exhaustion."*
> *—II Corinthians 4:1 AMP*

Write a Spiritual Goal for Readers

With your overall plan in mind, now that you have correlated the beginning of your book project with the end and reviewed your personal growth in completing this book that is designed to help other believers, pray for those who will be reading the book when it is published. Envision a particular audience, or perhaps several types of readers—young, old, male, female, American and in foreign lands. Pray for their enlightenment from reading your book, and that God's Word will become clear to them and manifested in their lives.

> *"But He said to them, I must preach the good news (the Gospel) of the kingdom of God to the other cities and towns] also, for I was sent for this [purpose].*
> *—Luke 4:43 AMP*
> *"He sends forth His word and heals them and rescues them from the pit and destruction [II Kings 20:4, 5; Matt. 8:8.]"*
> *Psalm 107:20 AMP*
> *"The Scripture says, No man who believes in Him [who adheres to, relies on, and trusts in Him] will [ever] be put to shame or be disappointed. [Ps. 34:22; Isa. 28:16; 49:23; Jer. 17:7.]*
> *[No one] for there is no distinction between Jew and Greek. The same Lord is Lord over all [of us] and He generously bestows His riches upon all who call upon Him [in faith].*
> *For everyone who calls upon the name of the Lord [invoking Him as Lord] will be saved. [Joel 2:32.]"*
> *—Romans 10:11-13 AMP*

Then write a short paragraph of a few sentences that describes your desired goal for readers—what is it you want them to glean from your book, and how can that help them in serving the Lord and minister to believers or unbelievers? Is there something they can learn that could be passed on to others, having a domino effect?

Finally, write a confession prayer for the readers who will encounter your book. Ask God's guidance to their hearts as they find understanding in your words about some aspect of their lives. Continue to pray for your readers, who will become your responsibility in your new ministry as a Christian author.

"For the kingdom of God consists of and is based on not talk but power (moral power and excellence of soul)."
—I Corinthians 4:20 AMP

Writer's Wisdom:
In completing my book, where does God want me to go from here with it?

For Revelation:
"Rendering service readily with goodwill, as to the Lord and not to men."
—Ephesians 6:7 AMP

The Master's Writing Plan Activities
Writing Step #1:
Review chapters five through eight, just as you did for chapters one through four last week, to confirm ideas, polish your style, and check accuracy. Print a copy of those chapters, and taking your time, closely again read through them to look for smooth flow of information and correct grammar usage. Use a pen to mark areas that need additional work. Or you can use your computer's editing function to make these corrections. Make an effort to improve something on each page. Even if you have thoroughly re-read the writing before now, there is still a good chance you can find things to correct or improve.

Writing Step #2:
Ask your reviewers or readers to supply a few sentences of summary about your book. Hopefully these statements can be used as endorsements on the back cover, to seek professional reviewers to read the book, and as copy for public relations materials, such as press releases or media kits. Keep a file of all feedback, even if you don't immediately use all of the comments, as they may come in handy later.

Writing Step #3:
Be sure to send a thank-you card to everyone who has read your book, or even just parts of it, and supplied feedback. The same holds true for any talks or presentations you are able to give to church groups, civic orga-

nizations, schools, businesses, etc. You are more likely to leave a good impression when you take time to be polite and say thanks.

New Testament Reading Plan Week #11:
1 Timothy through James

Chapter Twelve

Go Into the World

"And He said to them, 'Go into all the world and preach and publish openly the good news [the Gospel] to every creature [of the whole human race].'"
—Mark 16:15 AMP

As you complete Week 12 of the Master's Plan for writing a book in twelve weeks, you may experience a feeling of euphoria coupled with relief. On one hand, you have concluded a laborious task—writing an entire book in a span of about three months. On the other hand, your next task—looming perhaps larger and more daunting—is to get the book published and market it to an eager set of readers.

As discussed in the chapters that immediately precede this one, your first step now is to review the final four chapters and make sure they are ready for publication. You will need to follow the steps outlined in Chapters 10 and 11 for your book's first several chapters. Just as you did then, you should thoughtfully read over chapters 9 through 12, revise as needed, and try to find someone you trust to read those sections and provide feedback that will help you edit your writing to make it even better.

> *"A pupil is not superior to his teacher, but everyone [when he is] completely trained (readjusted, restored, set to rights, and perfected) will be like his teacher."*
> —Luke 6:40 AMP

Ensuring that your book is reader-ready will impress publishers or professional editors who may be assisting you with commercial publication or self-publishing. The less work they have to do, the more money you will save, and the better your book will be, since having done most of the writing and editing yourself, the book will reflect your personal voice and probably something of your personality, as well. Readers enjoy "meeting" an author through his or her writing, and they are delighted when they encounter interesting facts, humorous anecdotes, and Biblical principles that they can relate to and benefit from.

Final Format

After receiving feedback on the last four chapters, along with other comments or ideas that additional readers may want to share for the complete manuscript, you should begin organizing the manuscript into a publishing format. This doesn't mean that you have it type-set or arranged in printer-style layout as a "camera-ready" copy. Rather, it means that you finalize edits, proofread again to catch any missed errors, and select a professional format that will make the book easy to read for reviewers and editors.

Times new roman is a popular and readable style of print to use for a professional document, like a book manuscript. Courier and Arial also work well with certain types of documents, particularly play scripts and film scripts. Most editors like to see copies in 12-point font, with the text double-spaced throughout the manuscript. Here are a few other common conventions to consider:

1   Type on one side of sheet only.
2   At the end of a chapter, begin a new chapter on the next page.
3   Set up chapter headings uniformly throughout, i.e., 14-point font, bolded, centered, etc.
4   Insert page numbers only for the book's text, not the front matter (Table of Contents, Preface, etc.) or back matter (index, appendix, etc.).
5   Use black ink on-screen or in print.
6   If you print the manuscript, use 20-pound bond paper or an equivalent quality.
7   Avoid fancy drawings, insertions, or decorations, unless this is an e-book and you are knowledgeable about how to do them.

Overall, your manuscript should be easy to read, accurate, and unhindered by elaborate additions that will get in the way of an editor's prompt, comprehensive review.

The front and back materials referenced above can be added at this time. These will vary from one book to another, so give some thought as to which ones you actually need rather than simply adding them for effect. Depending on whether your book is fiction or non-fiction will impact which of these materials your book may need.

Front matter (materials):

1. Title page.

    This lists the title in large print, the author's name, and the publishing company.

2. Table of contents.

    This page lists chapter titles (unless chapters are simply numbered). There also may be a separate list of illustrations, photos, or other art work and additions, such as charts, maps, etc., although these are not always included in a list that appears in the front of the book.

3. Preface.

    The Preface provides an introduction to the book for readers, explaining its purpose or goal and what readers can expect to gain from it.

4. Dedication.

    Usually short, this page may list a very few names—usually God, family members, or inspirational sources—who helped to inspire the writing of the book.

5. Acknowledgements.

    This section usually consists of one to three pages listing people who were instrumental in assisting the book to get published. These may include reference persons, editors, proofreaders, secretaries, reviewers, sponsors, reference assistants, research aides, etc.

6. Foreword or Introduction.

    Some authors choose to open their fiction or non-fiction book with a foreword by the author or special guest, or with an introduction that offers background or supplemental information that leads into the main part of the book. This section, especially the Foreword, tends to be shorter than a typical chapter.

Back matter (materials):

1. Afterword or Epilogue.

   The author, editor, or another person may provide a short summary or follow-up to the topic in an Epilogue or afterword, which is optional, not mandatory.

2. Notes.

   These may be endnotes that simply list citations for numerical superscript textual references. Or the notes may be short paragraphs reference certain pages where additional explanation or background information is needed.

3. Works cited.

   For scholarly or journalistic books, and other kinds as well, you may want to list all the sources that are cited in the book. You should plan on following the relevant style guide for documentation style, often Modern Language Association (MLA) for humanities, the American Psychological Association (APA) for social sciences, and the Chicago Manual of Style (CMS) for journalistic types of books. There are nine or ten additional styles to consider, but these are the most widely used in their fields.

4. For further reading.

   This section, usually one to a few pages, lists additional books, articles, and websites that readers may find helpful on the topic of your book.

5. Index.

   An index is an alphabetical listing of major references in your book, such as key persons, historical events, special places, and so on. Whether you organize the index yourself or hire a professional indexer to do it, you should consider cross-referencing the most important terms so readers can find them more easily.

6. Appendix/appendices.

   Consider adding an appendix for large amounts of pertinent information, like a series of documents referenced in the book, a particular numerical system, alphabet or language code, etc.

Additional optional features include a list of characters for epic-scale fictional works. Any kind of special information that the reader may need to fully understand or appreciate your book can be included in a special format before or after the main part of the book.

Try to line up one or two reviewers to look over the entire book, once it has been assembled, to give you feedback on all the sections that you have included. These reviewers might be professional readers that you can locate on book review or publishing sites, or they could be friends who like to read and are good at it who can give you friendly advice about your book's readiness for publication.

Preparing to Publish

Today, in the early 21st century, numerous publishing houses abound in the United States and overseas, some of them quite large and prosperous by printing high-selling books in the millions of copies. Most publishers do not reach that level of profit, however. On average, they may offer an author a publishing royalty of 5% to 12% of the per-volume price. Some offer advances of $500 to $15,000 although it is possible for big-name authors to receive far more. (For more information on publishing advances, royalties, and related fees, check *The Writer's Market;* it is published annually, so look for the current edition. It usually takes a book between one and two years from the signing of the contract to reach book-store shelves during the publishing process.

"Thus says the Lord, your Redeemer, the Holy One of Israel: I am the Lord your God, Who teaches you to profit, who leads you in the way that you should go."
—Isaiah 48:17 AMP

Publishers designate a specific budget for marketing a book. Those funds can be used to ship free copies to teachers (for academic books), and reviewers (to get book cover blurbs and positive previews that will make people want to read the book). Other marketing costs include press releases, book store tours (though these have all but disappeared in late years), magazine and newspaper ads for your book, and special promotions, if applicable. When the marketing budget is depleted, the author will have to start plugging the book on his or her own, or hope that additional profits trickle in, if the book has benefited from publishing hype, or "buzz." Between six and twelve months after publication, the book more or less will have worn out its welcome, and be relegated to back stock or lower bookshelves to make way for newer books coming out.

> *"For not from the east nor from the west nor from the south come*
>   *promotion and lifting up. [Isa. 14:13.]*
> *But God is the Judge! He puts down one and lifts up another."*
> —*Psalm 75:6-7 AMP*

Based on this type of scenario, some books never "earn back" the advances paid by a publisher. Say, for example, you receive a $5,000 advance for your book, along with royalties in the amount of ten percent per copy. If your book is selling at $15 per unit (book), you will receive $1.50 per book. If total sales over the first year reach just 2,000 units, you will have earned back only $3,000 of your original $5,000 advance. Typically, sales slow down after the first year, and you may never earn back the advance you were paid up front. Consequently, that publisher may not readily work with you on future books. Other commercial publishers may be hesitant, too, if they find out your book did not earn back your advance.

> *"Therefore keep the words of this covenant and do them, that you*
>   *may deal wisely and prosper in all that you do."*
> —*Deuteronomy 29:9 AMP*

If you decide to explore commercial publishing options—that is, submitting your manuscript to an established publisher who pays royalties and possibly advances on the rights to publish your book, you can find valuable information in the annual *Writer's Market*. However, this section is devoted to helping Christian authors who are interested in self-publishing options for their work.

Self Marketing

Self-publishing has been around a very long time. In the days of the patriarchs, of course, it was the only way to get published. Hand-carving on stone or writing on papyrus were the chief ways of preserving important messages for large groups of people. Later, copies were hand-printed and distributed by messengers or caravans throughout the Middle East and beyond. We have much to be thankful for that those early believers zealously recorded and preserved their Christian legacy for future generations, including us.

Since the invention of the printing press several centuries ago, important documents were typeset and printed in a consistent manner that allowed for thousands of copies to be sent abroad and handed down from one generation to the next. Organized publishers who made a profit from printing the work of others did not really grow into a flourishing business until recent times. As discussed above, commercial publishing is not always lucrative for author or publisher, as a certain level of risk is involved.

"For as he thinks in his heart, so is he."
—Proverbs 23:7(A) AMP
"The thoughts of the [steadily] diligent tend only to plenteousness,
but everyone who is impatient and hasty hastens only to want."
—Proverbs 21:5 AMP

These are some of the reasons why more and more authors are choosing to self-publish their writing:

1 Author designs or assists with the book cover.
2 Author decides the number of copies to print in hard cover or paperback.
3 Author is involved with each step of the publishing process.
4 Author receives no advances, but will earn a higher percentage of royalties.
5 Author determines the marketing plan.

Self publishing can take many forms, including the following.

1. The author can set up a website for the book, promoting and selling it online.
2. The author can have hundreds of copies printed and sell them from home.
3. The author can utilize print-on-demand (POD), publishing copies as they sell.
4. The author can work with a distributor and a marketing firm to sell books to libraries, schools, bookstores, and other business entities.
5. The author can publish the book electronically as an e-book, or aurally, as an audio book.

Collateral materials can be ordered to promote the book via bookmarks, pencils and pens, candies, stationery, refrigerator magnets, and other merchandise, at additional cost.

The best way to decide how to self-publish is to survey several examples of self-published materials to get an idea of what they look like and how they are sold. You can find and contact self-publishing companies by doing an online search. You also may wish to browse self-published books at local bookstores and libraries that carry them. Or contact me at <u>www.writeitGod-sway.com</u> for information about our Christian community writers group.

Your Marketing Plan

Don't wait until your book is published to begin promoting it to the public. Your marketing plan should begin to be developed the day you decide to write a book. After selecting the type of book you will write and determine the probable reading audience, you will need to start planning how to get news of your book to those readers so they will want to buy it. The more attention you can bring to your book ahead of time, the greater number of readers you may possibly get.

> *"For which of you, wishing to build a farm building, does not first sit down and calculate the cost [to see] whether he has sufficient means to finish it?*
>
> *Otherwise, when he has laid the foundation and is unable to complete [the building], all who see it will begin to mock and jeer at him,*
>
> *Saying, This man began to build and was not able (worth enough) to finish."*
> *—Luke 14:28-30*

As mentioned in the last chapter, getting responsible people to review your book and write a short blurb of endorsement is an important first step. Try to make contacts with other Christian authors through websites, chat rooms, and discussion boards, and if you are fortunate enough to be in a writers' group, ask for feedback on your manuscript from the other members. This can be done by asking the group leader to designate a time when you can distribute copies for reader feedback or simply ask interested members if they are willing to receive a copy for editing. When this review is complete, and you have gotten helpful information about others' views of the book and possible edits that are needed, once these are made, approach the same reviewer or someone new to ask if that person has time to read and comment on your book for a cover blurb. These people will let you know if they are too busy or uninterested, so don't keep asking them—look for another reviewer. When someone does take time to read the book and offer feedback, even if it is negative, be sure to thank the person and send a note of gratitude to show your appreciation. They will remember it the next time you ask, and it's the courteous thing to do anyway. Don't be hurt or embarrassed by critical comments, especially if they are politely stated. Remember what the Book of Proverbs says about mutual edification:

> *"Iron sharpens iron; so a man sharpens the countenance of his friend [to show rage or worthy purpose]."*
> *—Proverbs 27:17 AMP*

Be grateful for honest comments that can help you make the book as strong as possible, even if that requires additional revision and editing.

> *"Where there is no counsel, purposes are frustrated, but with many counselors they are accomplished."*
> *—Proverbs 15:22 AMP*

Whether or not you plan to create an e-book, consider setting up a website that allows readers to see the cover, read excerpts, and order copies through your merchant's account. With a website, you have a personal bookstore that is open 24/7 where readers from around the world can shop anytime they want to. Make it easy for them to find information about your book by utilizing meta tags (if you don't know how to do this, ask a computer marketing specialist or borrow a library book on the topic). Write Anointed material for your web pages that will keep readers interested and encourage them to refer others to the site. Surveys, quizzes, and collateral materials for sale can increase interest in the website and help to build a solid base of support. Please visit this book's website for information about a helpful tip booklet on this topic: www.writeitGodsway.com.

Send a press release to community newspapers, ministries, and radio stations. Someone may want to interview you as a local author or expert on the topic. Register with Christian speaker's bureaus or contact civic groups like the Rotary and Chamber of Commerce; often these groups are looking for lunchtime speakers to talk about their book for perhaps 20 minutes, and you may be able to sell copies afterward, so try to bring a friend to do this for you while you finish your talk and answer questions. Also, try to be available to sign books whenever you sell them, as this helps to increase sales.

> *"Now when they saw the boldness and unfettered eloquence of Peter and John and perceived that they were unlearned and untrained in the schools [common men with no educational advantages], they marveled; and they recognized that they had been with Jesus."*
> *—Acts 4:13 AMP*

As you become renowned in your new ministry of expertise, the word will get out concerning your gift. Then, when you write another book, your name will be "on record" and people may be more apt to contact you for interviews or to give short talks where you can briefly mention your book rather than promote it outright. You may want to write a newspaper editorial on your topic, signing yourself as the author of your book's title. Or you may be able to create a weekly newspaper column on your topic by pitching it to the editor of that newspaper section, for example, health, Christian values, or visionary leadership, depending on your book's areas of expertise. The more your name goes public, the more likely you are to get known and sell books.

> *"While Peter was still speaking these words, the Holy Spirit fell on all who were listening to the message."*
> *—Acts 10:44 AMP*

If you are unsure about how to do these things or would like to go even further in promoting your book, consider hiring a public relations or marketing assistant. Paying for a few hours each week on a part-time basis for a month or two may be enough to give your book a helpful boost in reaching its intended audience. Visit www.writeitGodsway.com for additional information.

Trust and Pray

Although you naturally want your book to become successful and do its intended job, God knows best. It may be that the one or two readers it's supposed to reach will receive it, and in turn, go out into the world and carry your message forward in another format to a new audience. It's hard to know God's specific plan, so you will have to trust Him with the outcome.

> *"King Agrippa, do you believe the prophets? [Do you give credence to God's messengers and their words?] I perceive and know that you do believe*
>
> *Then Agrippa said to Paul, You think it a small task to make a Christian of me [just offhand to induce me with little ado and persuasion, at very short notice],*
>
> *And Paul replied, Whether short or long, I would to God that not only you, but also all who are listening to me today, might become such as I am, except for these chains."*
> *—Acts 26:27-29 AMP*

Pray each day for the book to fulfill its purpose. Again, you may not be sure how things will turn out, but God has a plan for your book. Having written, published, and promoted it, you can now sit back and wait to see what God does with it. The hard part is over; unless you find waiting to be difficult. Just do your part, and God will do His.

Be sure to give thanks that you have actually completed the goal of writing a full-length book. Many people aspire to authoring a manuscript, but only a small percentage achieves their goal. God is perfecting your life in a variety of ways, one of which undoubtedly is your newly written book. Rest in your newfound sense of accomplishment, and watch how the fruits of your labor bloom and blossom.

> *"A man's mind plans his way, but the Lord directs his steps and makes them sure. [Ps. 37:23, Prov. 20:24, Jer. 10:23.]"*
> *—Proverbs 16:9 AMP*

Writer's Wisdom:
How should I pray for my book's publication and marketing success?

For Revelation:
"Tell your children of it, and let your children tell their children,
and their children another generation."
—Joel 1:3 AMP

The Master's Writing Plan Activities
Writing Step #1:

In the last phase of the editing process, review chapters 9 through 12 to revise, polish, and proofread your writing, just as you did the last two weeks for chapters 1 through 4 and 5 through 8. If possible, get at least one other person to review the chapters and make suggestions for improvement. Implement the suggestions if you agree, and if there is time.

Writing Step #2:

Write a one-page summary of your book, as well as a press release. (You can find free templates and examples online by doing a search. Or visit www.writeitGodsway.com to review the list of supplemental materials that can help you take the next steps in getting your book published.

Writing Step #3:

Write a one- or two-page query letter that can be sent to commercial publishing houses or self-publishing companies, like Winepress Publishing (www.winepresspub.com) and Xulon Press (www.xulonpress.com), both of which are Christian self-publishing companies. My website likewise offers query help at www.writeitGodsway.com.

New Testament Reading Plan Week #12:

I Peter through Revelations 22

Epilogue

*"I will praise You, O Lord, with my whole heart; I will show forth
(recount and tell aloud) all Your marvelous works and wonderful deeds!"*
—Psalm 9:1 AMP

Give praise to the Lord that your book has been written! Without God's help, it would not be done. Without His blessing, it would have no meaning.

For many authors, completing a book is demanding and difficult. Puritan poet Anne Bradstreet compared writing a book to bearing a child, and everyone knows that labor pains are synonymous with suffering! Yet, I'm told there is no more fulfilling task than bringing a child into the world. So it is with laboring to bring a book to publication.

Now that your book is ready for the public, press on toward the goal. Read and follow the companion text, *How to Market a Book in 90 Days God's Way*, to get your message into the right readers' hands in a timely manner. The marketing workbook will lead you through important steps in self-publishing your book and finding its niche in the complex network of today's publications.

You also will want to visit this book's website for the latest publishing tips and guidelines provided by published authors and writing instructors: www.writeitGodsway.com. Take advantage of free, valuable expertise offered by successful Christian authors that can give you that extra edge and up-to-date information to get your book in print.

Although you have come a long way since God first placed the idea for a book in your mind, this is no time to pause in your writing ministry.

Continue to learn key aspects about the Christian publishing market and find out how to get your book into the mainstream bookstores and shops.

Above all, trust God to lead the way for your book's success. He knows what is best, and how your writing can be utilized effectively to help others. Continue to trust Him and seek His will. You won't be disappointed—and neither will your book's readers.

After-Words

"Every Scripture is God-breathed (given by His inspiration) and profitable for instruction, for reproof and conviction of sin, for correction of error and discipline in obedience [and] for training in righteousness (in holy living, in conformity to God's will in thought, purpose, and action)."
—2 Timothy 3:16 AMP

Now that you have worked through the process of writing a book in 90 days God's way, are you ready to have your work published? If you did not make it through the process completely, don't give up. Simply pick up where you left off, for example, in chapter four, and begin the process again with the goal of completing a chapter each week.

If that pace is too fast or you lack the time to develop your writing in a weekly chapter, adjust your pace accordingly. Learning the principles that are offered in this book is a good start toward writing your own book someday. Even understanding more about the Bible and how it is written for readers of all generations can enhance your personal devotional time for studying the Bible and the styles of writing that are used to deliver God's message.

"Study and be eager and do your utmost to present yourself to God approved (tested by trial), a workman who has no cause to be ashamed, correctly analyzing and accurately dividing [rightly handling and skillfully teaching] the Word of Truth."
—II Timothy 2:15 AMP

This speed writing method built on biblical principles can be used for many kinds of writing projects, not just books. If you need to prepare within a specific timeframe a sermon series, for example, or a compilation of devotionals, using the approach outlined in this book and addressed by resources found at our website (www.writeitGodsway.com) can help to make the task more manageable and meaningful. You can practice the writing activities at the end of each chapter in preparation for your next project. Or you can purchase related materials found on the book's website to expand your writing skills and experience.

Congratulations on taking this first giant step in your writing ministry! Continue to seek God's will for your writing by putting Him first each day in reading the Bible and praying for guidance. God will never let you down!

"This Book of the Law shall not depart out of your mouth, but you shall meditate on it day and night, that you may observe and do according to all that is written in it. For then you shall make your way prosperous, and then you shall deal wisely and have good success."

—Joshua 1:8 AMP

"All has been heard; the end of the matter is: Fear God [revere and worship Him, knowing that He is] and keep His command-ments, for this is the whole of man [the full, original purpose of his creation, the object of God's providence, the root of character, the foundation of all happiness, the adjustment to all inharmo-nious circumstances and conditions under the sun] and the whole [duty] for every man."

—Ecclesiastes 12:13 AMP

Sinner's Prayer

If you have found this book to be helpful, but don't know if your name is written in the Lamb's Book of Life (Revelation 21:27 AMP), now is the time to repent and repeat the following Scriptures:

But what does it say? The Word (God's message in Christ) is near you, on your lips and in your heart; that is, the Word (the message, the basis and object) of faith which we preach, [Deut. 30:14.]

Because if you acknowledge and confess with your lips that Jesus is Lord and in your heart believe (adhere to, trust in and rely on the truth) that God raised Him from the dead, you will be saved.

For with the heart a person believes (adheres to, trusts in, and relies on Christ) and so is justified (declared righteous, acceptable to God), and with the mouth he confesses (declares openly and speaks out freely his faith) and confirms [his] salvation.

The Scripture says, No man who believes in Him [who adheres to, relies on, and trusts in Him] will [ever] be put to shame or be disappointed. [Ps. 34:22; Isa. 28:16; 49:23; Jer. 17:7.]

[No one] for there is no distinction between Jew and Greek. The same Lord is Lord over all [of us] and He generously bestows His riches upon all who call upon Him [in faith].

For everyone who calls upon the name of the Lord [invoking Him as Lord] will be saved. [Joel 2:32.]"

—*Romans 10:8-13 AMP*

Name_____

Contact information_____

_____

Send a letter or email if you have been helped or ministered to as a result of this book.

Learn How to Write God's Way

**Henry Abraham's series on how to write and publish your work
God's Way can prepare you for a meaningful writing ministry with
life-changing potential!**

www.writeitGodsway.com

**Follow Henry Abraham's four-step process
to develop your writing gifts for the glory of God.**

* * *

**Find out how you can utilize your writing talent and
learn new skills to produce
a complete book manuscript
in 90 days.**

Step One:

Visit the Website

New and experienced authors can find valuable resources at our website:

<u>www.writeitGodsway.com</u>

Learn how to write effectively and efficiently from biblical principles that demonstrate God's perfect method of communicating with His people via the written Word—the Bible. Learn how to professionally plan, write, and edit your book to deliver a powerful message to readers around the globe.

At the Website, you can sign up for 12 weeks of free newsletters that are full of professional information and resources to keep you inspired and rejuvenated, spiritually as well as creatively. Explore topics like finding your spiritual purpose, choosing a topic, developing a focus, organizing your material, and considering your audience using proven methods drawn from published authors and writing instructors.

You can browse many helpful products and resources that are designed to encourage and support Christian writers. Take advantage of these special materials to maximize your talent and get your writing to the right readers.

Step Two:

Read the Book

Devote part of your day for the next 90 days reading a chapter from the book to learn how to become an effective Christian author. Written in an accessible, easy-to-read style, you will find countless tips and ideas to help jump-start your publishing ministry and get you over the hurdles along the way: schedule demands, satanic stumbling blocks, inexperience, and uncertainty.

Learn how to focus your topic, organize a table of contents for your chapters, and evaluate Web resources for accuracy and timeliness. You will be amazed by the practical biblical examples of written communication and audience awareness that are offered to illustrate God's way of writing to His people in the past and today.

Respond to the writing exercises at the end of each chapter so they can help you apply the principles to the practice of writing as you develop your book. With consistent effort each day for 90 days, you will experience growing confidence in your ability to put your thoughts into words that can be used by God to advance His kingdom!

Step Three:

Check Out Our Companion Products

How to Write a Book in 90 Days God's Way—
Companion Workbook (120 pp.)

    1   Follow prompts that will inspire creativity.

    2   Keep a journal of your book's development.

    3   Use the exercises when you get stuck.

How to Market a Book in 90 Days God's Way—120 pp.

    1   Become familiar with publishing trends.

    2   Learn about the publishing markets.

    3   Prepare your book for publication.

    4   Learn the 6 P's of marketing.

How to Write a Book in 90 Days God's Way—
Devotional & Bible Reading Plan (120 pp.)

    1   Chart a closer daily walk with God.

    2   Study the Bible for applicable spiritual truths.

    3   Follow the 90-day Bible reading plan.

How to Write a Book in 90 Days God's Way—
Writer's Journal (200 pp.)

    1   Record your thoughts each day.

    2   Explore your writing process.

    3   Keep track of budding ideas.

Step Four:

Additional Helpful Resources

1 12-week seminar: How to Write Book in 90 Days God's Way
2 5-20 page ebooks

1. How to write a query letter
2. How to find a publisher
3. How to find your book's marketing niche
4. 52 Ways to Self-Market Your Book
5. How to Write a Press Release
6. How to Request a Radio Interview
7. How to Get Your Book in the Public Library
8. 10 Tips for Scheduling a Book-Signing
9. 10 Tips to Get Your Book in the Newspaper
10. How to Get Your Book Reviewed
11. What to Do About a Negative Book Review
12. 5 Tips for Becoming a Public Speaker
13. 7 Tips for Selling Your Book after a Speaking Presentation
14. 6 Things to Keep in Mind About Your Book's Cover
15. 5 Overlooked Markets for Your Book
16. How to Assemble a Media Kit
17. How to Contact Radio and TV Stations
18. How to Prepare a One-Sheet
19. Interview Questions to Send Media Hosts
20. 8 Tips for Writing a Personal Bio
21. How to Generate Community Interest in Your Book
22. How to Reach the Christian Community with Your Book
23. 5 Tips for Writing a Doctrinal Statement in Your Book
24. Building a Website for Your Book
25. Promotional Tips for Marketing Your Book
26. How to Write an Accompanying Workbook
27. How to Establish an Author's Profile
28. Planning a Speaking Tour
29. Negotiating a Publishing Contract
30. Basic Guidelines to Understanding Your Publishing Rights

Appendix

To the Introduction

Writing Schedule Worksheet

The following questions will help you think through your daily schedule to find time for writing your book over the next 90 days.

1. What is the best time of day for you to spend time alone to work on your book?

2. Try to narrow this period of time to a general set of hours, for example, before I go to work, sometime between 6:00 p.m. and 9 p.m., or right before bed.

3. Check your calendar or planner and pencil in tentative writing times, working around special events like vacation, visits, etc.

4. Designate a secondary back-up writing time of about two hours daily in case unexpected interruptions delay the process. Keep this time-frame in mind for future reference.

Choose Your Book's Topic

In addition to the description of your book that you summarized at the beginning, use this page to explore the topic you plan to write about. Consider this a worksheet of ideas that does not require firm answers. You can experiment with an outline, drawing, or list of ideas to help you think about the book you want to create.

Fiction Novel:

Character List

If you are writing a novel, list your main characters below with a paragraph of description about each, following the example. Be flexible, knowing that your character might change as the story evolves. But for now, these details will help you begin to create realistic figures for your story.

Example:

Peter Jarrell:

Peter is the 37-year-old former pastor who left his church due to growing self-doubts. Thick dark hair and piercing brown eyes get him noticed in public. Separated from his wife and nine-year-old son, Peter takes a job on a warehouse loading dock to keep physically busy and avoid thinking.

Fiction Novel:

Plot Structure

List the main characters' actions that you are thinking about using in your novel with the understanding that these could change later. This is just a draft of ideas for now.

Example:

1. Peter Jarrell preaches a powerful sermon, only to be challenged by a mysterious visitor afterward. Losing his confidence, his resigns from the ministry.

2. Separating from his wife and son, Peter takes a manual labor job to avoid painful memories. He begins to go to bars and adopt an immoral lifestyle.

3. One dark night when he is about to carelessly drink more than he should and get drunk, the same mysterious figure appears to challenge him again.

Non-fiction:

How-to Book

To write a how-to book, begin by asking a question or describing a problem. You can practice doing this several different ways to get the focus that you want for your book. You may end up writing about one of these questions or address several of them in your book.

Example:

1   How can parents get teens more interested in the Bible?

2   How can teens be inspired to read the Bible more often?

3   What are some things the youth pastor can do to encourage teens to read their Bibles?

Preparing to Start

In addition to following the start-up steps outlined in the early chapters of this book, think of things going on in your life that need to be addressed before you start writing.

For example, is your ministry preparing to embark on a building fund drive? Are you busy with the Missions Board? Are you enrolled in a schooll of ministry? Below in the space provided, list any considerations or competing commitments like these that could delay or interrupt your book-writing process.

Example:

1. Wait until our church launches its building drive.

2. Seek a temporary replacement for my position on the Missions Board.

3. Complete the current semester or course.

Notice to Family and Friends

Although it may not be necessary, depending on how extensive your social commitments are or how often people contact you and their reasons for doing so, you might want to draft a short note explaining that you are writing a book for the next 90 days, which is making a claim on your schedule until such-and-such a date. Using a friendly tone and offering to get in touch later, your note will kindly alert others to your increased busyness and perhaps defer non-critical issues until after the 90 days. Keep the note handy for quick emails or greeting cards, amending as needed.

Example:

"Thanks for getting in touch! I've been thinking about you and would enjoy getting together sometime in three months or so, when my current project (or book manuscript if you want people to know) will be finished. I'll be in touch then—looking forward to it!

In the service of the King, (your name)"

Launching Prayer

As you prepare to launch your 90-day project, first pray to God, explaining your hopes and desires, as well as asking His blessing and guidance. Writing your prayer will keep it handy for later references when needed.

Example:

Dear Father,
    I am unsure about how to go about writing my book, and I ask for Your help in meeting my goal in 90 days. Please clear my mind of distracting thoughts and help me to fulfill other commitments while taking on this one, too. May the work of my hands glorify You in everything that I write.

In Jesus' Name

Biblical Revelation

The Bible is full of inspiring stories, people, and events. Briefly describe one of your favorites that perhaps has helped to influence you to write. Then meditate on why it is part of the Bible and how it continues to help readers today.

Example:

The Apostle Paul wrote the Book of Romans to encourage believers in the city of Rome. Though he was a prisoner, Paul carefully and logically outlined the plan of salvation to make it clear for those who were unfamiliar with it. Because of his commitment and writing style, countless readers have come under its influence to be saved and to share their faith with others.

Logical Thinking Exercise:

What role did writing play in Jesus' life?

Christians think of Jesus as the Master Teacher, and indeed He is, especially to the people of His time when He interacted with them personally. Jesus knew the Scriptures thoroughly, no doubt in part from His divine nature. But did writing (and His reading of it) influence Him? And did He ever write while on earth? Exploring these questions will help you to think about Jesus' personal relationship with reading and writing. (This is a good warm-up activity for a day when you have writer's block in working on your own writing!)

Example:

Jesus may have read the Scriptures for Himself as opposed to hearing them taught in the synagogue. He also might have written something of meaning when He stooped and wrote in the sand when the adulterous woman was brought for condemnation (John 8:3-11).

CPSIA information can be obtained at www.ICGtesting.com
Printed in the USA
BVOW02s1607211113

336840BV00003B/931/P